A JAILBIRD'S-EYE VIEW OF TENT CITY

By
Di Erickson

Artwork by Rob Bouchard a.k.a Cactus Bob, Phoenix Arizona

ISBN-13: 978-1495267956
ISBN-10: 1495267954
BISAC: Humor / Topic / Political

PROLOGUE

This tale takes place in Tent City, also known as ItsHella Jail, located in Phoenixville, Arizona. It is a story, albeit sensationalized, based on real events, real people, and a real place. Names have been changed to protect the guilty.

My name is Janie Doughy. I'm about your age, a backsliding Christian, drug abuser, and thief. It is that last bit that got me into trouble. However, crystal meth deserves an honorable mention. I credit methamphetamines for giving me the wherewithal to do stupid things quicker and with more enthusiasm. Left to my own devices, I find myself behind bars. This is where imperfect people end up, where rock bottom rises up to meet us. A jail sentence was the best gift the authorities could have given me. The time I spent in jail was the most crucial period of my pointless life.

I spent twenty years climbing utility poles and splicing cable for the cable company. We all know that television is a conspiratorial device of mass deception. Commercialism is the curse of the age. It pains me to admit that I've been conspiring with the enemy.

Fascinated by all things electronic, I studied electrical engineering. I'm two semesters short of a B.S. degree. When I think of my gargantuan student loan my stomach starts to hurt.

Thus far, my life is a flop. It is as if I had spent decades groping about in the pitch dark, only to switch on a light to find myself no further now than the day I graduated high school.

Locking me in a cell and telling me to STAY was just the thing I needed to keep me from chasing my bungling tail. I'd discover that I'm not an Engineer. I'm just a scheming working class girl at heart. I wasn't so different from my new criminal cellmates with their neck tattoos and half shaven heads.

This place offered real promise that I might get better, at getting worse. I devised all kinds of tobacco related capers, turned bread crumbs into wine and learned how to light a cigarette from an electrical outlet, all the while becoming a degenerate gambler. I don't mean to glorify incarceration. I'm just saying one shouldn't knock it until one has tried it.

I was remanded to the ItsHella County Jail's indoor lockup for a period of six months while public officials leisurely mulled over my case. I was convicted of this and that, and then sentenced to serve one year in tent city.

This jail is run by the legendary lawman, Sherriff Joey Porcupino, the self described "Toughest Sheriff in the Cosmos" and a virtual pioneer in the field of public accommodations. Sheriff Porcupino is a virile brute of a manly-man who is hardly a homo, despite his perverse fascination with men in pink undies. His name is known nationally and is synonymous with such terms as corruption, incompetence, and Homeland Insecurity.

Too old to be in jail, too young to die of old age. I'm forty-eight.

PART ONE
INDOOR LOCKUP

ONE

Karen was the first of many cellmates that I'd encounter. She's in her mid-forties and looked like someone's sexless mother. She has nice teeth, good posture, and a generally pleasant outward appearance. Upon closer inspection, I'd discover that Karen looked upon all fellow inmates with utter disdain. She'd put-on a great air of dignity as if her being here was some grotesque accident. She spoke with the noblest contempt, turning her nose up, affecting so lofty a manner that all who dealt with her were tempted to punch her face.

The reason for Karen's incarceration was a mystery. If I had to venture a guess, I'd say she's here on attempted murder charges. She had threatened to kill me and she seemed comfortable with the exchange. She did so in the voice of one midway through a prizewinning exorcism. Her threat was an angry response to my insistence that she shower.

Oh, didn't I tell you? She stank. It was a foul odor rotten enough to stifle breath. It was the smell of everything being perfectly wrong.

It is disconcerting to gulp in the vile fumes of the unwashed. Her stench was always present and made worse with her every movement. It was as if her body was providing the service of trapping the odor but could only do so much. Even when she left the cell, which was seldom, the smell remained on her bunk lofting upwards as if longing to escape and return to its source.

I found myself trying to inhale in small, shallow puffs of air in an attempt to safeguard my internal organs. The odor was heavy, persistent, and   so potent that it could be detected from the outside of our cell by anyone walking past.

The cell we shared measured twelve feet by eight by twelve high. It had the feel of what it must be like to live inside Tupperware. What these cells lack in space, they make up for in a lack of privacy. The floors are gray cement. The stockade, like in most institutions, was calculatedly dingy. The off-white cinder block walls were blotted with poop, snot, and graffiti left behind by disenchanted inmates. The cheerlessness about the interior might invoke a gloomy effect if you hadn't the conversation of some of the more amusing residents.

Summing up, it simply didn't have the look of a place where something good might happen. The intrinsic charm isn't a thing that strikes you immediately. You have to let it grow on you.

Each bunk offered a wafer thin mattress, one sheet, one blanket, and no pillow. The pillow is a dangerous weapon. There are no mirrors. This is a good thing. As I plunge into the vast wasteland that is middle age, I've noticed that mirrors aren't made with the same high quality that they used to be. Mirrors of old provided a softer more flattering me. Today's mirrors are the enemy of dreams.

At 2200 hours, the cell doors are electronically locked and remain so until 0900 hours. During the day, we were free to roam from our cells to the dayroom. Smelly never left the cell unless she was making one of her mock phone calls.

Two phones are mounted on the wall in the dayroom for outgoing calls. Inmates are only permitted to call collect. These phones were switched on and off via controls in the guard station which is commonly referred to as "the bubble". Loopy made her calls when the phones were off. She typically made a spectacle of herself. Today was no exception.

"Get me out of this hell hole." She bellows into the dead receiver. Her mental patient hand violently slaps the concrete wall.

"They are trying to break me. I've been beaten, anally molested by a broom stick, and made to drink my own urine."

"I'd love to meet that broomstick," a woman said in obvious poor taste.

Many thought this was hilarious which stirred up a wave of giggles.

"I've been subjected to every kind of mistreatment these monsters can dish out," she says while eyeing the crowd to insure her psychotic episode isn't in vain.

"I can't brave this storm much longer. Money is no object." She finishes the presentation by smashing down the receiver like a fricken lunatic. Every tirade ended with 'money is no object'.

Because there is so little to do in lockup, many looked forward to this continuing saga. Explosive episodes are the kind of distractions that relieve monotony. Onlookers would shake their heads in amazement while looking sympathetically in my direction. Their pity did help. I always feel better when people feel sorry for me.

When the carnival sideshow is over, Karen sits in the dayroom. She holds herself upright with an air of stiff back confidence. Her pointy chin is tilted high hinting at the possibility that she had formerly been well off.

"That was our family's attorney," she announces. "I'll be leaving this God-forsaken-place shortly."

"If only this were true." I'd lament loudly hoping to stir up more sympathy.

Karen was as crazy as a loon. I can ignore this. The occasional Linda Blair impression, albeit disconcerting, was easily overlooked. However, the contemptible odor was more than I could bear.

It was week two into this cellmate arrangement when, much to my horror, I was bullied out of my slumber by odors from the abyss. I woke to a startled and defenseless nose. Her foulness had ceaselessly been angling to setup shop in my nostrils. Now it had succeeded. The smell was like a kick in the face. The offensive fumes caused my eyes to water. At any moment, I was half expecting to see a swarm of flies.

The thought that I had been breathing in this defiled air throughout the night made me want to vomit. I quickly covered my nose and mouth. I found myself becoming terribly agitated. I've had enough! This is why I hate people. Finally and with suicidal clarity, I knew what I must do. I'd stop the next guard making rounds and plead for a relocate. A decision made with some trepidation knowing that complaints, if handled, were done so with severity.

The guards make their rounds every hour on the hour. The sound of clanging keys announced her arrival. I sprung into action. I approach the on duty officer with soft eyes and a warm smile. I was hopeful to enlist her humanity.

"Excuse me, Officer."

She stopped and looked at me stone faced and tight lipped.

"Yes, good morning, Officer." I clear my throat. I'm feeling a little nervous. "I'd like to request a cell reassignment. Is there a form I need to submit?"

"No." She briskly walked around me.

I followed.

"Excuse me, Officer. I'm afraid I don't understand. No, there is no form or I can't be reassigned?"

"No to both."

She was moving forward with no intention of stopping. I was hot on her heels picking up my pace to meet hers. This was beginning to piss me off. I tried being civil. It was apparent that courtesy was wasted on this Nazi.

Perhaps I should exercise some compassion. I had read somewhere that a government job was the closest thing on record to a near-death experience.

She was moving briskly toward the large Plexiglas sliding door that the guard in the bubble was beginning to open for her electronically.

My self-control, so sorely tried, fractured. Against my better judgment, I went off, like a bomb.

"I won't spend one more day breathing in the vile stench of that self-deluded mental patient!" I cried out. I was red faced and foaming at the mouth.

The officer stopped, turned, and smiled a smile that was harder to bear than a shovel to the face, somehow.

"I don't know what you're talking about."

"You know darn well what I'm talking about." I bawl.

My voice is squeaky with pitiable emotion. My words a cry of anguish forced from the depths of my core. I felt as if all the rudimentary decencies of life were being sullied.

"IT ISN'T FAIR!"

Now I'm sniveling. I have successfully reduced myself to a three-year-old.

Outrage vibrated from my every pore. Our eyes met in silent conflict. I wanted to pull her hair until she cried.

I had made a stupendous fool of myself. I can admit that.

9

Take it easy, I lectured inwardly. Breathe and pull yourself together for God's sake. I was being toyed with. The officer did understand my situation. Her resistance was due to the bottom line. We had a full house and stinky had to be somebody's albatross.

I apologized for my outburst. I did so in a mumble, briefly, and with no real contrition.

I forged ahead with a new and improved strategy.

"I'd like to submit a formal grievance, Officer. My cellmate has threatened to kill me."

"Kill you?"

"Yes, Ma'am, 'stab me to death in my sleep' is how she put it. Surely, you have some obligation to protect inmates who receive death threats from the criminally unhinged."

"Do you wish to be placed in P.C.?"

"Yes," I said enthusiastically. Relief reshaped my face.

"No."

Now she's wearing a smirk.

I closed my eyes briefly. I counted as high as seven then with calm, I met her gaze.

"No what, Officer?"

"Do you know what P.C. means?"

"No, Ma'am. I do not."

"It stands for Protective Custody," she said in a tone of amusement. "You just agreed to be put in the hole."

The officer looks up at her coworker in the bubble who's shaking her head in disbelief. She's tuned in electronically and can hear everything that's being said. The consensus is that I'm an idiot.

"Fine, put me in the hole. I'd agree to a public lynching to escape that rancid cabbage smell."

I sensed the possibility of resolution nearby. I raise a forefinger, "just one second, please."

With small hope rising, I made a beeline for my cell. Holding my breath, I gather my bedding and Bible. Faster than you can say "You smelt it. You dealt it." I stood before the guard once more.

"I'm ready, Officer!"

A soft smile played on the officer's wooden face. She looked perfectly human then, an awkward, decent woman in a man's unflattering polyester uniform no doubt issued back when she weighed less.

"Put those things back into your cell. Your concern will be addressed."

I stood before her with a look of skepticism. She returned my look with one that suggested I do as I'm told. I did.

On her next round, the officer carried a fresh set of institutional garb. She stopped into our cell and tossed the stripes to stinky ordering her to shower. Stinky complied.

Everything was roses and lollipops for about three days. When the effects of the shower wore off, so did my happiness. Stinky was released the following week. I thanked God.

TWO

A thick manila envelope was delivered to my cell. It would be the first of three separate indictments I'd receive. What I know of the rules of law would easily fill a thimble. I didn't know what an indictment was. It seemed to be an official script chocked full of indeterminable muckity muck.

I'm not a complete moron. I pride myself on being of at least average incompetence. I remember seeing a summary of someone's interpretation of our judicial system that seemed to sum-up what part I understood:

The Assertion below is TRUE.
The Assertion above is FALSE.

I've never cracked open a law book in my life but I've seen plenty of television. I think it has provided me with a solid frame of reference in which to validate my fear.

The State prosecutors operate from a staggering lack of harmony. They are working from a different sheet of music than the rest of us while insisting that they aren't. Gazillion new laws are written daily that they take particular care to multiply, whereby wholly confusing the opinion of fact and fiction, right and wrong. It is a system so torturous and convoluted that a mere human is considered a fool if they should attempt to defend them self.

Long before I was caught, I had the look of an escaped convict, lurking in bushes, convinced that I was being followed. Somewhere there existed a warrant that bore my name. I was sure of it. The anticipation had ruled my life. My arrest was a welcomed relief.

It was time to pay the piper. I just needed to know how much. I've been here two months with zero understanding of the magnitude of my impending disaster. Finally, they send me a clue.

I read the indictment several times with all the comprehension of Morris the Cat examining the nutritional data on a box of 9Lives. The whole of it was disconcerting.

There comes a time when one must put their trust in a higher power. Only I remembered that I didn't have my laptop and couldn't get to Google. Instead, I'm forced to turn to a more seasoned inmate who knows the ropes.

I decided to take my paperwork to Tami in hopes of some clarification.

Tami was a miserable piece of work. I've met skinheads with personalities that are more agreeable. Her attitude was largely hostile. Everything about her seemed unbearably smug. She had an inflated self-esteem and was vain for no discernable reason. She was no beauty, as I may never tire of pointing out. The fact is she's utterly lacking in feminine allure, possessing all the sex appeal of an orthopedic shoe, yet her utter averageness seemed arrogant.

Tami had the air of a woman who was thoroughly at home. She's a perfect example of the eccentricity of the inmate population. Many here have fallen into a dreary pothole of existence and have given up on being normal or civilized. Incarceration frees them from appropriate standards of behavior just as death might free one from a miserable life.

I wondered if I might become like her. I had changed a great deal from the frightened girl who entered this ward a couple months ago. All that once bewildered has become ordinary and routine. I know the detention officers that are safe to approach and those to avoid like a colonoscopy. The familiar sound of their boots as they make their rounds, the rattle of their festooned hardware, the exact time they will reach my cell, and whether or not to feign sleep to avoid having my bunk tossed. The thought of this is half gratifying, half disturbing.

In short, I've become as naturally at home and familiar with this place as if I had been born and raised here. It is a frightful realization that my nature is capable of so much degeneracy as to make pleasant and agreeable, that which is an utter disgrace.

Tami was seated at a table in the dayroom. She was alone. As I walked toward her hostile and suspicious presence, I began to feel uneasy. I have a history of shrinking to arrogance and found myself wrestling with that now.

"Pardon me." I said meekly.

She wasn't defensive exactly, but she declined to look at me.

"I don't mean to be a bother."

I watched her bitch eyes look up from a trashy romance novel.

"Then don't be."

She went back to reading.

I'm quick to take a hint. I'm generally able to spot when my presence isn't desired. Reading between the lines, I could see that she was wishing me elsewhere.

Well, she has some nerve. Did she honestly imagine that I was so easily put off?

More superior human beings than she had tried to get rid of Janie Jane Doe Doughy and were forced to admit defeat. What of the service of common courtesy anyway? Such deeds of kindness have fallen on hard times in our day. Her foul, unforgivable nature didn't discourage me. Being an advocate for civilized behavior, I pressed on.

"I'm not leaving until you take a look at these."

I extended the arm, paperwork in hand.

She looked at me as if my mere existence was reason for me to apologize. This wretched crone was steeped in unwarranted importance. I forced myself to ignore her self-imposed celebrity status. I was more interested in her help then her approval and felt some comfort in knowing that one day she'll die.

I take a step forward.

"Just a quick look, please."

She paused reflectively and placed her book on the table. Then she took my paperwork, more out of vulgar curiosity than courtesy. Eyeing the documents, she pressed her lips together and shook her head in disapproval.

"This is some shit."

Her observation wasn't only unhelpful but uncalled for. I was hardly surprised at her shocking lack of taste and decency.

Although I'd never wish a hideous flesh-eating disease on anyone, some do seem to be asking for it. I struggled to overlook the vulgarity. Patience, I lecture inwardly, give yourself at least one virtue.

"Do you think you could be a bit more specific?"

"Could you be a bit more specific?" She parroted sourly.

She was mocking me. I was beginning to hate her. I count her my enemy. She gave me a look that said the feeling was mutual. Our views on each other were definite.

With a great deal of bitterness Tami concluded, "You're screwed, specific enough?"

"Thou hast also given me the necks of mine enemies; that I might destroy them that hate me." Psalms 18:40, Halleluiah!

It would appear that neck wringing is scripturally sound. God is good. How I'd love to give her neck a speedy one hundred and eighty degree twist. I had my fill of deadly insult. A girl can only take so much.

I don't mind telling you, every time Tami gave that condescending glance then turned away as if it disgusted her to look at me, a tinge of anger burned in my belly. I came within an inch of occupying the top story on the ten o'clock news as the latest killing sensation. There was a moment when I could almost see the headlines:

"TENT CITY INMATE GETS IT IN THE NECK." When asked what prompted the gruesome slaying the perpetrator responded, "I'm hoping this will count toward my community service hours".

Giving her my acid glare, I gathered my paperwork, turn, and go. And to think I wasted my good manners on her. This degenerate gives me reason to rethink my position on abortion. She's proof positive that it is never too late.

This vile splotch is a threat to homeland security. For the sake of the future of humanity, I hope this social parasite of the lowest and foulest order is never released.

+++

15

I haven't always been a loser. I'm not a career criminal. I graduated High School in 1979 then joined the Military. After a four-year hitch in the U.S Army, I attended one of those trade schools that specialized in electronic repair. I landed a job with the cable company were I stayed for nineteen years. I worked in the field, splicing fiber and coaxial cable, repairing plant outages, balancing amplifier cascades and whatnot.

In 2002, I was making a decent wage and content in a six-year relationship with my girlfriend, my soul mate, Nikki. Then one day, rather unexpectedly, I find said soul mate in bed naked with my best friend. The thing threw me for a loop. It left me in a long-term stupor. I should have snapped out of it. I did not know how. I generally have a thick skin unless it comes to matters of the heart. Then I become a retarded marshmallow.

Soon after that karate chop to my solar plexus, I was fired from the cable company. Then, I lost my house and rental properties to foreclosure.

I found myself on a sinking ship. The harder I tried to scoop out the water the more aggressive the hole became. At some point, you have to let it go. So, I said screw it. I got terminally, high and became a burglar.

I've always felt more comfortable on the wrong side of the law. I started shoplifting at a very young age, like many, only I never stopped. Burglary seemed a natural progression. I'm not proud of this.

Such is the nature of sin, I suppose. When it has made a home in us, it is hard to shake. Once we're hard-boiled in crime, no fear can affect us; no good example gives us reason for self-reflection. Bad behavior is a habit we create only to find soon after that the habit creates us. John 8:34 puts it simply; "Everyone who commits sin is a slave to sin."

I'm reminded of my last law-breaking debacle, the one that landed me here. This was in mid 2005. Most of my break-ins were carried out between two and four in the morning. I only hit construction sites and select commercial enterprises that I don't like. I always worked alone.

Burglary requires boldness of the most caste iron description. It is a task best preformed while sedated. Fortunately, I had become a full-blown meth addict.

I suppose I was walking up and down in front of that construction site for an hour before I could bring myself to approach the fence with my trusty bolt cutters. Even then, I crouched before the fence for about thirty minutes cowering against it, listening for wailing police sirens. Eventually, hardening my thoughts against all fear, I summoned the nerve and got down to business.

Chain link fences are hardly the pinnacle of safekeeping. They are often secured with a lock that can be opened by anyone with a hairpin. Bolt cutters are quickest and work like a hot knife through butter. The proprietor might as well hang out a shingle that reads, "Break and Enter". A thief is a creature that watches the advantages of other people's mistakes. Criminals are inherently lazy. If things are made even the least bit inconvenient for us, we move on to an easier mark. This has been a public service announcement.

Once the hole was big enough, I low-crawled through to the other side. Aside from the loss of an inch of skin from my back, everything seemed to be in order. I was apparently alone. Here I was in a place the cops will soon refer to as 'the night in question'.

I noticed some cameras but saw them as largely ornamental for I came dressed for the occasion. A disheveled bearded homeless man with abnormally bushy eyebrows will be their culprit when they rollback that footage. Just adjacent to the cameras on a nearby lamppost sat an owl that was staring down at me with a great deal of dislike and suspicion. I was startled by its presence and obvious lack of hospitality. Avoiding the owl's gaze, I summon additional courage, drew in a deep breath, and started to navigate the site.

I saw twenty company vehicles and a couple of tractors. The utility cabinets on the work trucks always contain a cornucopia of pricey hand tools. If the bins are locked, no problem, these are simple pin-and-tumbler locks and are frightfully easy to open using a pick and tension wrench. As luck would have it, I had a set in my truck.

As I walked back toward my truck, I noticed in a corner of the yard, a shitload of gas powered commercial grade jackhammers. Holy Mackerel, I hit pay dirt. I saw dollar signs. There must've been thirty of them right out in the open, so to speak. I only needed a few.

This caliber of demolition gear is easy to unload and a steal-of-a-deal at two hundred dollars a pop. It would cost more than that to rent one for just one day. There was a minor hitch. These monsters weighed-in at about ninety pound each. This was just a little less than my current body weight. Could it be that my eyes were bigger than my upper body strength?

No worries. I mustn't be diverted from a task by petty trifles. I had read somewhere that ants can carry ten to fifty times their own body weight. Nearly all the ants you see in the wild are female. "And by gum, so am I!" I encourage myself.

Am I not smarter than an ant?

"No stupid!" cried my inner saboteur.

"Screw you!" I holler back appearing rather mentally deficient.

I needed a snort of redemption, liberation from my in-head succubus. The most efficient way to get rid of my demons is to do a big fat line.

I made a beeline for my truck, slipped into the cab, and carved out a couple big fatties. I angle the straw up against my nose and gave a quick sharp inhalation through one nostril. First the burn, then an immediate chemical taste at the back of my mouth, and then the sweet satisfying sense of relief. I sighed pleasantly.

The treatment worked like magic. The effect was far from disagreeable. Two doses of this miraculous remedy and cripples fling their crutches and dance the polka.

What they put into the stuff besides rat poisoning and maybe anthrax, I can't say. It thoroughly altered my outlook on life. In the blink of an eye, it makes everything more compelling to the point of captivating. That white powder not only eradicates my worries, but it also gives me what comfort there is in the illusion that nothing matters. It should be illegal to feel this good. Oh, right, it is.

All better, I head back toward the site. Looking up, I caught the owl's hypercritical stare. He sat in judgment. His was a look that rankled. I raised myself to full stature and narrowed my eyes at him to show who the Alpha was here. He seemed unmoved by my bravado. Owls aren't so smart. I tried to convince myself. Ignoring the birdbrain, I rolled up my hobo sleeves and got down to business.

By way of sheer determination, ample amounts of blood loss, and more than a few tears, I managed to get two jackhammers onto a portion of ground just behind my Nissan pickup. From this point, what remained was a piece of cake.

Two weeks ago, I had installed an electric winch to lend a helping hand with those things that were not so easily portable. Putting in place a couple of two-by-fours, I attached the winch cable to each jackhammer. With a push of a button, each gizmo, in its turn, was properly stowed.

All things were in their place and I was ready to go. I got back in my truck, removed my ingenious disguise, mopped the brow, and turned the key in the ignition. I was merrily on my way contemplating the windfall that was fated to grace my very near future.

I didn't travel more than three-hundred yards when there on the roadway, as if waiting for me by appointment, sat five police cars. Their lights were ablaze and several officers were outside their vehicles with weapons drawn.

What a gigantic coincidence. What're the odds? Instinctively, I put on my seat belt and tossed my drugs out the window. My mind reeling, I stopped the truck on the centerline and wondered how I might get myself out of this fresh new hell.

It was an embarrassing moment. Blinded by spotlights, I couldn't see him. But, I could hear the footsteps of the officer coming toward the vehicle, accompanied by the unmistakable sound of a gun leaving its holster.

I wasn't sure how to start the conversation.

"Oh, well, there you are, Officer." I say to the muzzle of a handgun.

"I was just about to call you guys."

"Is that right?"

"Yes, Sir, I noticed a suspicious character lurking around a construction site just down the way."

"A suspicious character you say?"

The officer's flashlight beam came at me like an accusing finger. The light searched the inside cab then with a flick of the wrist the beam moved elsewhere. He was swept the light through my camper shell window.

"Plan on making some road repairs?"

"I'm sorry, Officer, I'm afraid I don't follow."

"What's up with the jackhammers?"

"Those belong to my friend."

"A friend you say?"

"Yes, Sir, I just borrowed his truck so that I might take some can goods to the homeless shelter to feed the starving orphans."

The Policeman regarded me with what seemed to be amusement.

"Oh sure and Mount Rushmore is a natural rock formation."

"It is? I did not know that!"

"Get out of the vehicle and put your hands where I can see them."

This was my clue that the jig was up.

I was cuffed, read my rights, and placed in the back seat of the police car. Not a word was spoken all the way to the station.

I surmised that this is customary when one is caught dead to rights. I guessed too that the whole thing was probably on blue-ray DVD by now ready for its label "STATES EVIDENCE, EXHIBIT: 'ALL WE NEED' and slated to be shown to twelve angry men.

After considering the condition of my current affair, my heart struck a new low. I was on my way to the place that had so long expected me and that I had so long evaded. I was waist high in the soup and sinking deeper with each passing mile marker.

I was feeling like a passenger of the S.S. Minnow on a three-hour tour--a three-hour tour. It is all over, I felt, except for the composition of lies in which I'd confess everything.

My brief run-ins with the law as a juvenile taught me that law enforcement agencies are hardhearted machines that once set into motion disregards nearly all causes. They refuse to accept shattered hopes and dreams as an excuse. One won't get terribly far pleading 'it was the day before my period' as mitigating circumstances for breaking and entering. Surely, they won't give a rat's ass about my girlfriend's infidelity or the properties I lost to foreclosure.

I found myself regretful. Not because I was a lying thief. Not because I had forsaken my fellowman or that, I was a bitter disappointment to my Maker, my Mother, and myself. None of these things came to mind. I regretted that I had thrown those drugs out the window. I should've swallowed that baggy.

+++

I was interrogated once I reached the station. I found this to be an unpleasant ordeal for which I was ill prepared. There was the small matter of those darn jackhammers in the back of my truck. An assortment of burglary tools were yet another disconcerting factor. It would've been easier to explain the discovery of my girlfriends decomposing cadaver. Who doesn't understand how trying a relationship can be?

Detective Sherlock was a stern woman, all business, and no bullshit. I don't mesh well with the authoritarian type. The whole of her appearance was that of a woman designed to instill law and order to the nth degree. There was something severe and laugh-less in her manner, rather steeped to the gills in serious purpose.

She wore a man's white cotton dress shirt, black slacks, comfortable black leather loafers, and a thick black belt festooned with a holster and firearm. This outfit could cause anyone to appear butch. Detective Sherlock was tall, big-boned, but not fat. She wasn't ugly but she wasn't attractive either. She was rather plain with all the sexual allure of ringworm.

As I reclined in the electric chair, the detective turned up the juice. Her eyes beamed through me like a couple of death rays. She scared me. The Detective regarded me with a great deal of disapproval. I could read what was on her mind as clearly as if she had been rude enough to scream it. She thought me a loser.

21

That would make two of us. This is precisely what I had decided while en route to police headquarters. Tending to be fair minded I didn't blame her for holding this view.

She drew in her breath sharply and I could see that my stock had plummeted several more points in the negative. She's a woman of elevated moral fiber and purpose. I'm just the type of uninspired and frivolous nuisance against which she's most likely to be prejudice.

"Mother Teresa of Calcutta," the detective said in a tone so cold I could have sworn I saw her breath.

I stared at her blankly for several seconds. My neck was stiff. I rolled my head from side to side a couple times and heard this crackly noise. I definitely needed a massage.

Then like a bolt of lightning, the thing comes to me.

"Oh yes, Detective."

I was responding to the alias that I almost totally forgot about. They were insistent that I give them a name. Mother Teresa was the only one I could come up with in a pinch.

"Do you think we're a bunch of idiots?"

The Detective's lips took on a sneer. The eyes were two glassy dots of festering disgust.

Sherlock Holmes himself might've been misled, but I see there was no getting a thing past this woman. Struggling to display no weakness, I respond in earnest.

"Well, Officer, it isn't that obvious to the casual observer…"

Thinking better of it, I switched gears and decided to ask a question that I had been mulling over on the way to the station.

"Before I incriminate, or worse, embarrass myself perhaps you can tell me just how far one can stretch the truth before it qualifies as perjury?"

The Detective flashed me an intense and terrifying stare. Her face, like a slab of granite. She let out a snort of contempt.

I firmly shut my mouth. I'm afraid the little I said may have been too much. Her posture was an equal measure of offense and irritation. I see now my question was not a good one.

Her expression suddenly changed to a serious-matter sad smile. "We know who you are, Doughy. We've had you under-surveillance for the past six months."

It took several seconds for the full horror of these words to penetrate my foggy control center. The words "cumulative" and "evidence" sprung to the mind. The thought of this had all the effects of a bad hit of acid and a kick in the stomach delivered simultaneously. For an instant, I had forgotten how to breathe. I had been under surveillance. Of course, I knew I was being watched. That wasn't just my imagination after all. Ha, ha, see, just because you're paranoid doesn't mean you're not being followed.

A hard glimmer had come into the detective's eyes. She had the look of a cat whose paw was on the tail of a mouse.

My eyes fell to the tabletop. I felt the will drain right out of me. No doubt, the detective will judge my entire moral backbone on the wide-ranging data they have amassed. This impending massacre was beginning to have a damaging effect on my marginal self-esteem. All my sense of worth nosedived plummeting from barely to zero in a split second. Her meager opinion of me was working its magic. A little more of this and I shall become flattened, a mere human splotch.

I've been around long enough to know that you can't make her kind take the romantic view. Definitely not the sort of girl I felt I could open up to. I could see at a glance that this woman wasn't going to be an easy audience. It is darned difficult to appeal to ones better side when one has none. I'd need to watch my every word. Unpleasant life experiences have trained me not to show my ignorance right up front.

The severe detective was standing with her back turned. She was facing a large mirrored window when she spun around unexpectedly and fixed me with a challenging stare. The look made me realize what a black crow must look like to a little baby worm.

"We know your crimes are gang related. If you give up some names things might go easier for you."

I was less than pleased with the tone of this objectionable exchange. Furthermore, I didn't like her attitude, although I felt that this wasn't the moment for saying so. I decided to counter her

23

accusation with muddled irrelevance. Leaning forward, I spoke directly into the tape recorder on the table.

"I'd like to shift the focal point of this conversation to my rap sheet, Detective." I stated with a look of innocence.

"The fact is I have no prior, Officer. I'm a patriotic American with a solid work history, I happen to keep a lovely lawn, and I am a member of AAA. I have the gold membership. I'm a model of respectability whose motives are as pure as the driven snow. My past can bear the strictest investigation. I'd be happy to get you references that will provide striking testimonials to my intrinsic worth. I don't think it'd be overdoing the thing to say that I'm the milk of human kindness, just the salt of the earth."

I'm not entirely sure what that last part means, but I'm confident it needed to be said. This should be the crux of my defense. I'd stick to my story with the tenacity of an able-bodied leech.

The Detectives eyes were icy and indecipherable. I bore her gaze like a dentist's drill. She was an expert at the trick of quick diagnosing of character and what she saw of mine didn't electrify her.

"Let us talk about those jackhammers," she said finally. "And what of these other things we found in your truck?"

She stood and removed a clear baggy from her pants pocket and threw it on the table.

"They look a lot like burglary tools, wouldn't you agree?"

She sat back down with an air of cocky reassurance. Resting her chin on her fingertips, she leaned forward with expectancy.

This naturally opened up a new line of thought.

I winched as I eyed the collection of tools that were placed before me. I could feel the look of pain flitter across my face. I lowered my eyes   like   a   nun   before   the   Holy   Mother. It came to me in a sickening thud. I must appear terribly guilty.

My eyes fell on a memorable set of lock picks and homemade jiggler keys that I had painstakingly created with my beloved Dremel tool. Tension was mounting in response to mounting tension. I was beginning to feel how scared I should be. By degrees, my situation became clear and I considered it with all the foulness of a lucid mind.

Now might be a good time to consult my lawyer. Only I don't have a lawyer. I'll be assigned a public defender. Many believe that they need a good lawyer when what they really need is a good judge.

The whole "public defender" sham is suspect. The county will provide an attorney who works for the county. Naturally, these folks are duty bound to do the will of the county. The phrase "conflict of interest" springs to mind. These legal professionals find themselves in a catch- 22. They can serve God or money. According to the Bible, you can only pick one.

All this thinking is turning my mood a misty bleak. Fresh beads of sweat were rolling down my forehead. I noticed that I had been grinding my teeth. Shivering attacks began followed by cold sweats.

I must've looked like crap. If this Detective had a shred of compassion, she would've known I needed a fix or a nice nap. I theatrically padded a yawn to extinction, but still the Detective seemed oblivious.

Gang related? This allegation is preposterous. The only street gang I'm familiar with is on Sesame Street. It is true that I'll steal anything that isn't firmly fastened to the wall, but I'm a lone wolf. I've always gone to great lengths to avoid people. A gang, being plural, is completely out of the question.

I was in desperate need of a restorative. I was experiencing the full effects of methamphetamine withdrawal. The symptoms include brutal irritability, dry mouth, drug cravings, deep dejection, paranoia, panicky nausea, and sweating. I had them all. My tongue had swollen into a family size bag of cotton balls. I could feel an immense grinding weight on my shoulders. It became increasingly difficult to pay attention. I slipped in and out of a deep mental fog. I found myself daydreaming that I was a lab rat using my hairy little paw to push the button that doled out more cocaine.

"So," said the sleuthhound with fatigue and annoyance prominent in her voice.

My mind had been wandering, as it so often does, but her magic word brought me back.

I pulled myself together with a visible effort. I concluded that the Detective must've said something before the "so". I didn't hear her. I totally forgot she was in the room.

I was about to respond "so, so what?" But then I thought better of it. Instead, I came back with the old cryptic standby.

"Huh?"

The narrowing of eyes told me she wasn't impressed.

Thinking fast I said, "I was told there would be doughnuts."

The Detective said nothing.

"If I'm expected to stay the night, I'll need some jammies and a toothbrush."

"You aren't leaving this room until you give me something I can use."

Her hands gripped the table edge, as she half reclined in her metal chair rocking back and forth on its hind legs. She had the air of a woman who had no place else to be.

I'll just bet that they lied to me about the doughnuts.

"Fine," I said in defeat. "I can't take one more nanosecond of this Chinese water torture. I'll give it to you straight."

I saw in her steely gray eyes a tiny flicker of relief. I couldn't help but feel happy for her. She did all that was in her power to bring me to my knees; to turn grayer the hair and multiply the lines that graces the face of this, your humble correspondent.

It was high time she got her due. This woman obviously deserved a break already. She has no doubt worked hard to achieve rank and prestige in this male-dominated profession. It would not kill me to throw her a bone.

"I'm working under the auspices of the federal government." I confessed openly.

The Detective's lips curl up in a smile that didn't seem to reach the eyes.

"This is all classified and I regret to say, I'm forbidden to discuss anything further without permission from my superiors."

"What superiors?"

"I'm afraid I've already said too much."

I buttoned my lips with my thumb and forefinger making a production of throwing away a key.

The Dick exhaled sharply through pursed lips and flared nostrils. She looked exhausted.

"I'm done with you."

Not for nothing, I've had my fill of her too. I like to think with all this time wasted that they have at least been getting my room ready.

She pushed herself away from the table as if she were pushing a mountain just a couple inches forward. Once erect she turns toward the door and leaves the room.

Boy does she have a lousy job.

THREE

Required court appearances are typically thirty days apart. Those with a scheduled court date are roused to wake at 0200 hours and tossed a fresh pair of stripes so that we might look our best. Between 0200 hours and your appointed appearance time, often midday, was the most hated stretch of this process. One hundred or so inmates assemble sleepily into the long corridor while we wait for our name to be called.

When summoned, we moved like cattle two by two waiting for our turn to be shackled in pairs. Both hand cuffs and leg irons are used. The uber-bad girls go solo and sported waist chains as well.

This was standard procedure for transport to another location. The courthouse is located approximately five miles from the compound.

On my first, of what would be seven, trips to the courthouse I had been shackled to Sarah. She was here on child molestation charges.

Sarah's face was Casper white, abnormally long, and thin. Her teeth and gums, being too large for her mouth, were the kind that took over the face. Two narrow chicklets protruded outward making one wonder if her top and bottom lips had ever actually met.

It was completely impossible to look at Sarah and not think of Mr. Ed, the lovable talking horse. In fairness, it was hardly the girl's fault that her face resembled a weary mare. Certainly, this wasn't something that she could have chosen for herself. Still, being this close to Sarah's unphotogenic horse face was rather off-putting. Her alleged pedophile charges didn't help matters.

Sarah spoke in a dreary muffled monotone, inserting apologies before she needed to make them. Her voice, like salt to an open wound, sucked all the joy out of what might otherwise be a shared camaraderie. A bore in the habit of exhausting her listeners, Sarah never shut up. Her company left one longing for a vaccination against dullness.

I had always thought myself clever. I was proud of my ability to make people go away and this is my punishment.

Once shackled, we're loaded onto a bus. Climbing in with leg irons attached to a fellow inmate was a little tricky. The shackles were comfortable, apart from my perverse longing to cross my legs now that I couldn't.

When we were settled into our seats, I noticed that for one split second Sarah had stopped talking. With her free hand, she reached around herself and tugged on my sleeve. Minding my manners, I bravely faced her with a polite empty expression. I prepared myself to be bored.

"I'm sorry and what was your name?"

"You can call me Wilber, I jest."

She didn't get it. Apparently, she doesn't have Nickelodeon.

"I'm sorry, what?"

"Never mind."

"I didn't touch my daughter," she began in a horse whisper.

Lookie here, I wanted to say. Who cares why you're here and you ought to be in a circus with that face.

I'd read somewhere that it takes less energy to be polite than rude. Still it's exhausting.

It must be about three in the morning. I'm not a morning person. I sat in a stupor hardly registering the sexual deviant's unsolicited life history.

Sarah didn't seem to desire nor expect a response. It seemed enough for her to be talking. This one-sided discussion was weighing me down. My head began to feel terribly heavy. It began drooping like a wilted tulip on a stem. I start dozing off, tumbling into that half awake, half asleep state.

Secretariat, either not noticing or not caring jabbered on. Her voice was a steady drone lulling me into a pleasant slumber. Suddenly, I find myself back in my cell comfy, cozy, and snug under scratchy wool. I sigh pleasantly. This is more like it. I breathe out a sigh of gratitude. This must be what heaven feels like.

Leaning over to check on my bunky in the cot below, I lose my balance. I felt myself falling, falling, falling... I jolt upright to stop from hitting the cement floor. I blinked twice. Befuddled, I look around.

That's when I realized; I'm back on the bus shackled to Sarah who was still talking.

I began to feel like a fly stuck to a strip of sticky paper. Sarah droned on, conversing with the seat in front of her as if it were a studio audience.

"My husband was molesting my daughter," Sarah said, "it started when she was six, she's nine now. My sister threatened to call the authorities if I didn't put a stop to it. We all knew it was happening. My father did it to me when I was her age. It's just a thing that happens."

"Not to everyone." I said.

Sarah looked at me as if I had just told her that the Earth was flat and I could prove it. She squinted causing the lip to rise showing more incisors than I wanted to see. My input had caused a brief lull in the conversation, very brief.

"I was always afraid to speak up to my Dad. I couldn't stand up to my husband either."

Sarah looked like a scared little pony. I found myself feeling sorry for her.

"My sister turned us in. When the Police came for my husband, they brought me in too. I was charged with aiding and abetting. I'm an awful coward," Sarah admitted. "I should've protected my daughter. I've been weak and scared all my life."

Sarah's face went cloudy with a chance of showers.

Uh-oh, I didn't like the turn this exchange was beginning to take.

"I'm such a terrible, terrible person." Sarah owned up.

Struggling with her emotions, she began to cry.

"Ahhhh, geeessss." I pleaded. "Don't cry!"

Thanks to her blubbering, I was on the verge of tears.

"Please don't cry!"

I wasn't sure if these words were meant for her or me.

Sarah's face compressed with the promise of more tears.

Oh for God's sake! I don't need this crap. My face registered annoyance. This is precisely why I hate people.

"I'm sorry," Sarah said.

She was patting her eyes with her sleeve, trying to pull herself together.

"I'm sorry, Wilber. Really, I'm very sorry."

It is in situations like this that I can feel the strings of my upbringing jerking me back. I hadn't been raised to embrace, or console, or to become a part of someone else's problem. I had been raised to mind my own business and to keep to myself. My layer of polite interest had worn thin.

I quickly ran out of sympathy.

Obeying the pained look on my face, Sarah shifts to a lighter subject.

"So, what're you in for?"

I raised my unshackled wrist to a clear line of sight. I look at my opened palm lovingly with merry eyes twinkling.

"I killed my entire family with my bare hands."

Then I turned to Sarah and gave her a look edged in ice.

Sarah's eyes grew to the size of soup bowls and her mouth dropped open. She swung her horse face forward and not a whinny was heard from her all the way to the courthouse.

Oh sweet peace.

+++

Heaven quickly turns to a more familiar wretchedness once you reach the courthouse. From the hustle, bustle, and fevered activity of the transport, one might suppose that our court appearance was scheduled for one hour past our rising from the rack. This isn't the case. We arrived at the Court House just after three in the morning. This gave us eight whole hours to spare before our eleven o'clock appointment.

This isn't unlike being in the military. I noticed the tendency on the part of both agencies to start missions off with a whoop and a holler and then sort of lose interest. Hence, the expression known to every veteran, "hurry up and wait".

We're herded out of the bus, marched through an underground parking garage, and taken to holding cells located in a dimly lit basement.

These cells provide tight sleeping quarters and are curiously suggestive of a rat hole. This environment is but a step removed from the dungeons of medieval times. Each cell contained four wall mounted metal double bunk beds, two on each wall on both sides, leaving a very narrow thoroughfare in between. With sixteen inmates to a cell, it offered the accommodations of a filled-to-bursting point Salvation Army collection box. The cells are ice cold and the bunks narrow without mattresses.

Four to a bunk puts us so close to one another that no air could come between us. Chill from the metal rack radiates through the fleshy tissue straight to bone. Death and the ever-lasting agony of hell would be more enjoyable. It would be warmer. Some women spoon each other for heat. This was a flagrant violation of my personal space and need for civilized distance.

I pressed my back against the frigid cement wall in an effort to avoid personal contact. The wall made my back numb with cold. I shiver violently while struggling to control the chatter of my teeth.

Sleep is impossible. On subsequent trips here, I'd put on two sets of jail wear to counter these arctic temperatures. Guards demanding excess clothing are removed before leaving the compound thwarted each attempt.

I noticed the girl on the top bunk just across from me. She glanced longingly at the stainless steel commode that was sandwiched between the cell wall and the foot of the bunk.

She jumped off her bunk, looked at me apologetically.

"Sorry, I gotta go".

Oh no, not that.

She quickly dropped her pants and plopped her posterior down on the john. She used the lavatory loudly and abundantly. It then turned out that the flusher was defective and the cell stank abominably for the duration of our stay.

We all lay there trembling and steeped in stench for an estimated four to six hours. The perceived length of detainment was right around forever and a day.

The court appearances consisted of a room full of fifty or so sleep deprived inmates. We all stare straight ahead hollow-eyed and jack-jawed, wearing the look of doomed passengers on a sinking ship. The participants are both male and female.

We're seated in metal folding chairs facing an altar-like structure. On top of this structure, there is a television. Inside that television is the judge, which left the viewers to imagine, if one could, the full majesty of justice.

A jailer stood reclining against the edge of the altar tapping his chin listlessly with a large skeleton key. Television court proceedings don't afford the innocent a chance to explain how the whole arrest thing was just one of those laughable misunderstandings.

When your name is called, you stand at a podium. In the time it takes to receive Holy Communion, you're back in your chair with another court date thirty days out. This information could easily have been scribbled on a post-it and stuck to our cell doors, sparing us the horror of transport while saving taxpayer dollars. Despite the venture, nothing is gained.

For the return trip, we don't go back to the dungeon of dread. Instead, we're taken to the "blue dick room". Here we wait for the bus to take us back to ItsHella.

This temporary holding tank has all the ambiance of a sleazy nightclub restroom with a fraction of the square footage. It offers standing room only with a sardine style, stuffed to exploding point type feel. In this room, we're so close and so many that I thought I might suffocate for want of air.

This chamber gets its name in honor of the large penis drawing that grace the blue solid steel cell door. It comes complete with testes and sperm droplets. The scratch art is a deep etching produced by some form of forbidden contraband that the artist should never have possessed and which lends to its enduring charm.

The wait in this holding cell is usually only a couple hours. By this time, you'll find yourself longing for the isolation of your cell and your bunk with its wafer thin mattress that would be considered an insult to offer to a visiting relative. The dime store yoga mat and scratchy military blanket you once turned your nose up at is now the sole object of your desire, making evident just how relative all things become.

FOUR

Maria is an attractive Hispanic woman. She is in her late thirties and has the look of a wild child whose been sobered by time and tragedy. She's as tough as a restaurant steak with a face as serious as a tax audit. Hers was strength built not on success, but on failure. A kind of steely fortitude one develops by ceaselessly swimming upstream against a merciless current.

Maria is a motherly, interfering kind of woman with a lifetime habit of butting into other people's business. Righting even the slightest injustice, she was the picture of vigilance. A helpfulness that when persevered became impertinence. A helping hand that looked more like homicide.

Typically, Maria keeps to herself standing on the second tier looking down on the group like a lioness might look upon her cubs. She surveyed her domain with the severe focus of someone who knows what's best for all and would not hesitate to let them know. When she observed a situation that she perceives as unjust, she moves in like a testicle tethered bull determined to set things right. The day I watched Maria dislocate a fellow detainee's jaw was the day I placed my designs on her to be my new best friend. Not in the habit of seeking out friends, I decided one should be enough.

The girl Maria popped had ripped a page out of the Book of Mormon to use as a rolling paper for the tobacco she had scored. This is no doubt the worse kind of sacrilege and it pains me to say, it is common practice. A heartfelt apology goes out to all LDS church members who might be justifiably outraged.

Maria is a mother to four strapping teenage boys who she adores. Before her arrest, she had been living with them and Bobby, her boy toy -- 20 years her junior -- who "screwed me like crazy", her exact words. Maria has been married four times and Bobby was slated to be future ex-husband number five.

Maria insisted on providing endless sorted details about her sexcapades. She believed the greatest form of complement to be the male erection. I'm rarely interested in the sexual going-ons of others or myself for that matter. Much of what she delighted in describing left me with a sour stomach. I had said to Maria, "The next time you think to explain your sex life to me, I'd rather you set me on fire then walk away."

She thought I was kidding.

Maria is here on solicitation charges. She has been here before. Prostitution is a misdemeanor until about the fourth or fifth time through the system. Then it turns into a felony. They call it a sex crime. Such an appropriate pairing of terms as is often the case with sex. It is never as wonderful as we imagine it'd be. There's the real crime.

The majority of prostitutes here will perform a blow job for a dime bag, but more often will settle for a couple of cigarettes. Those women who demand respect for their expertise and agility in this chosen career black hole (pardon the pun) refer to themselves as Escorts.

Can anyone tell me why prostitution is a crime? It is a thankless job. An occupation that some men find so amusing, a commodity, but the compassionate woman sees it as an abyss of misery. A profession that forces one to caress the ugliest of salivating primates. Some of which have careless habits of cleanliness. These men sicken a woman of delicate taste. Women of the night, as they are so called, are exposed to every unthinkable insult and outrage. Theirs is a shit job. They should be duly compensated. Let's call it what it is, a field position in Human Servicing. I say we make it a government job headed up by the Department of Erections. These girls are entitled to a decent salary with medical, dental, and a double-dip pension as afforded "the good old boys". Let's throw in an Emmy for good measure. That's all.

+++

It is after 2200 hours, lights are out in the cell, and the cell door is locked. I don't have a bunkmate. Oh happy days. Because I took a long nap earlier in the day, I'm not tired now. I can get light enough to write if I sit on the floor by the door and use the light that filters in from the dayroom. The key is that I must get back into my bunk when I hear a guard making rounds.

If they find me awake, I'll be sent to the dayroom and they will proceed to toss my bunk. When I return my cell will look like it's been hit by a tornado. If they find something they shouldn't have, I'll wish I'd been hit by a tornado.

I'm sitting on the floor, my back against the wall; my legs are stretched out in front of me. I had just finished writing a letter to my Mom. I was placing it into an envelope when I feel something crawling along my leg.

I look down and smile. Just above my knee sits Fertie. He's on his haunches, his little paws are in receiving position, and his anxious raisin eyes are looking up at me. He's so cute. I met Fertie the first week I was here. We became fast friends.

"Hi, Handsome, are you hungry?"

Of course, he's hungry. He's always hungry. I gather Fertie in one hand and used the other hand to help myself up. I place him on the small square stainless steel table and sit on the stool. Reaching into the trashcan, I retrieve some green bologna from this morning's provisions. I give a pinch of meat to Fertie. He takes a bite and tucks it into his cheek.

"You know, Fertie, I've got myself into a spot of trouble that I can't see my way out of just yet. A need for immediate cash has put me neck deep in the soup."

Fertie looked at me with a great deal of compassion and understanding. He's a good listener.

Recent rotten luck has put me in the rears with Hennessey, the in-house bookie. I owe her ten bucks, plus a twenty percent penalty charge. It's not a lot of money unless you don't have it and have no way of getting it. In which case, it may as well be the Dead Sea Scrolls.

Now every time we pass each other, Hennessey gives me the toxic stink-eye. I find myself avoiding her like that name I can't pronounce.

Most of life's pesky predicaments are easily resolved by simply running away. Jail doesn't offer that option. It is not like I can slip out the back, Jack. Make a new plan, Stan.

Hennessey corners me in my cell yesterday.

"Hey, Deadbeat, your account's in the rears, I need you to settle up."

I just stood there with a frozen smile that had no effect on her. I wasn't keen on the name-calling but I didn't say so. When she gets like this, I find it difficult to breathe.

For crying out loud! What in the heck happened to the spirit of mutual trust? I mean to say; I intend to pay her back. Golly, if you think nobody cares just try missing a few payments.

Rising from my stool, I place a toppled over cup by the door and sit on the floor. My back is against the bottom bunk, Fertie's at my side.

I give the verbal command 'Fertie, go' and he runs across the floor and into the cup. Turning around in the cup, he comes back and I give him a bologna treat. We can do this for hours.

"Fertie, go." I say again and off he went.

In the past four months, I've tried to teach him other tricks like sit, play dead, and fetch the guard's keys, etcetera. "Fertie, go" is the only one he gets.

As I watch Fertie coming back for his reward, my mind reels about my financial dilemma. I just need to play a few fast hands of poker, double up, and catch-up. I regard gambling as a prudent and conservative investment. A few profitable games and I feel sure I'll be back on top of the world looking down on creation. This thought made me feel better.

"Good boy, Fertie." I filling his little paws with the green stuff.

When I finally worked up the courage to speak to Hennessey I say, with downward eyes, "owing to the circumstance of my being fiscally crippled, I'll have to pay you on Friday."

"Okay, Doughy. Here's the deal. I like you, but I can't take the insult. I'll throw you a bone just this once."

"Oh, thank you, thank you."

I'm pathetic.

"Here's what I can do. We can put your joint-by-joint dismemberment on hold. I'm afraid we will have to impose a twenty percent penalty. Unavoidable administrative fee, you understand."

And I did. I understood I bought myself two more days. I almost gave Hennessy a hug and then remembered we were in jail. Instead, I jumped up and down gleefully and clapped my hands. Hennessy gave me a look that suggested this wasn't the thing to do either.

I must confess I was sweating bullets. Every time someone owes Hennessey money some nasty mishap occurs. You can predict the thing with absolute precision. This leads me to believe that it may not be mere coincidence.

Hennessy and I are about the same height but she's ten years younger and has zero body fat. You can't trust a woman that thin and muscular. It is simply not natural. Personally, I think she is an android. I'll lay odds that if you peel back that hairline you'd see a circuit board.

In short, she's a powerhouse of raw force who could make mince meat out of me by thinking it into reality. Hennessey is a cordial gal until you're in default. Then she takes on the air of a highly decorated Sergeant First Class.

"You're such a smart boy, Fertie."

He nibbles his treat. All this thinking is making my stomach hurt. The sound of footsteps on the stairs announced a guard approaching.

I jumped up and slide under my covers. When the coast is clear, I fall back to the floor. I look at Fertie.

"You're not tired of playing yet?"

I give the command, "Fertie, go."

He ambles toward the cup. I smile as I watch his hind end toddle. My boy's getting fat. I may need to find a bigger cup. I watch as he exits the container and trots back. That's when the penny dropped.

The solution to my problem was staring me right in the face.

"You're my ace in the hole, Fertie."

With hope rising, I placed a stamp on my Mother's letter and slide it under the door. The next passing guard will pick it up. I climbed up to my bunk and say a prayer. I was out like a light.

+++

39

Joy had cometh in the morning and in prosperity, I shall never be moved. Read that in Psalms, somewhere. Turns out, it was true. I was brimming with the hope of possibility. I was feeling chipper than whatnot. Something good was going to happen today. I rose cheerily to welcome the first day of the rest of my life.

I sat in the dayroom patiently waiting for everyone to finish his or her morning provisions. When all were sated, I stood on a chair and called the room to order.

"Get off the chair," bellowed a hostile voice through the PA system.

I got down.

No worries, I had everyone's attention.

I've managed to develop a decent rapport with the girls in this ward. My being here for four months made me one of the senior residents. This gave me some clout. Most found me amusing and amusement fosters liking in return.

"I have a proposition for those savvy investors in this room." I said with the air of collusion.

Then in a smaller voice, as not to be heard in the bubble, I said, "For those interested in a lucrative side bet, see me in cell numero ten, second floor."

As if they didn't know.

"Now what?" a skeptic cackled.

"All I'm saying is you snooze you lose."

I made my way up the stairs.

Maria popped her head out of her cell as I passed by.

"Now what the hell are you up to?"

"This one can't miss." I said. "This idea is going to catapult me out the red and into the pink."

"Uh-oh, this can't be good."

"Your lack of faith in me stings, Maria."

We both turned to see six women headed up the stairs.

"This better be good, Doughy," the fat one said with labored breathing.

"I endeavor to satisfy."

I pulled a face at Maria.

"You see, these women have faith in my genius."

Maria rolled the eyes.

"Poor misguided fools."

This is a woman with some nerve. For now, I'll let that remark slide.

Maria followed me to my cell. Six other women were right behind us.

I crawled under the lower bunk to retrieve Fertie. He hides here when I have company.

"You're going to have to trust me on this one Fertie, I need your help."

I emerge with Fertie in hand. Two of the girls screamed bloody murder. You'd have thought I had threatened to poke out their eyeballs with the sharpened end of a toothbrush. They went barreling out of the cell in abject terror.

"No need for alarm." I say. "This is Fertie. If you're uneasy with mice we can pretend he's a hamster."

Maria, having already met Fertie, was grinning ear to ear.

"Is Fertie a part of your big idea?"

"As a matter of fact he is."

I wasn't sure I liked her mocking tone.

The other girls stared with a mixture of skepticism and curiosity.

"On command, Fertie will go into a turned over cup six feet away and then come back to me."

"Bullshit," cried a cynic.

These words were music to the ears, a balm to the soul. My thoughts sang hosanna.

"No bullshit. In fact he will do it three times in a row."

"I'd like to see that," said the fat one. Her hands were on ample hips. Her facial expression was rather smug.

"Care to wager a bet? Risk a little. Win a lot. I cater to the naysayer. One commissary item gets you a ticket to play. Now go, Ladies. Spread the good news and prepare yourself for A Really Big Show."

The girls chuckle and leave the cell.

"You're out of your mind." Maria said. "If you need money, I can lend you some."

I raise both hands.

"I don't need your money, Maria. I'm telling you. I've got this one in the bag."

I kissed Fertie's little fuzzy head and let him scurry back under the bunk.

"We've practiced this routine for months. We have the process down to an exact science. It can't miss."

Maria sighed heavily and went back to her cell.

Maria is a remarkable woman. However, she can't always see the spacious, bigger picture.

The girls were all chomping at the bit to get a piece of the action. As each entered my cell with a commissary item, I wrote down who gave what. They received in return a square of paper with the words "FERTIE EXTRAVAGANZA" written in bold pencil.

Fifteen in all signed up. The game is double or nothing. If Fertie does as I publicly announced, they get nothing, nada. I felt no need to consider the alternative. I had this thing sewn-up with the jackpot money as good as lining my pockets.

Hennessy will be paid back and I'll never go through a bookie ever again. I think.

It's my faith in good luck that has always sustained me. I was bloated with the prospect of splendid fortune. I see now I may have gotten a little carried away.

The lucky participants insisted that the demonstration take place in the dayroom where all fifteen eager audience members could witness 'The Amazing Fertie' in comfort. My cell was just too small to accommodate an event of this enormity.

The whole dayroom was electric with anticipation. I placed the turned over cup on one side of the dayroom. Walking backwards, I estimated a six-foot distance from the cup. I sit on the floor placing Fertie by my side. Ticket holders gathered and gawked. It was time to get this show on the road.

"Master Fertie works best in complete silence." I say in my announcer voice. "Please take a few steps back. You're crowding us. It's especially important that you all shut your pie holes. Fertie and I appreciate your cooperation, thank you."

Since these girls don't seem to know what 'shut the pie hole' means, I had to endure snickering and chatter. A stern look on my part called these barbarians to order.

When you could hear a pin drop, I placed "The Stupendous Fertie" into position. I took in a deep breath and centered myself. With a dictatorial attitude, I gave the command.

"Fertie, go."

Fertie seemed desirous of moving toward the cup but was experiencing some trouble. He would have a speedy go of it then drawback. He stood on his haunches shooting quick glances left then right as if dreading the examination of the public eye. Fertie's little whiskers waved through the air wildly. My frantic little buddy was beside himself.

I hadn't seen this coming. The change in setting obviously threw Fertie off his game. The presence of a mob was the other factor I failed to consider.

I used to have the same trouble when I played basketball. On the playground, alfresco, I was can't-touch-this invincible. I'm not one to brag, but it has to be said. I was a street ball Goddess of the highest bust-a-move order.

BUT, when you put me in the shout-filled space of a gymnasium with those shiny wood floors and bleachers full of hypercritical gawkers, I froze up. You would've thought my nimble fingers had never met a basketball.

I tried to explain things to the girls. I attempted to shine some light on an angle that they might not otherwise grasp. I meekly suggested that a bit of patience was necessary due to hostile surroundings. This brought on a wave of hysterical laughter.

"What an idiot," said a cackling sub human.

"Oh my God," cried the sub human's relative as she blotted her stupid drippy eyes.

"Make her stop. I can't breathe."

Once again, I find my noble dreams are thwarted by some trifling particular. Ignoring the hyenas, I pick up Fertie.

"It's okay, Sweet Boy. It's not your fault. I understand."

I put him down and gave him a whole piece of bologna to make him feel better. Grabbing it with his teeth, he struggled to drag the greasy tripe to a quiet corner.

The girls seem to find this even funnier. Fertie and I had become a laughingstock.

"I'm Sorry, Fertie." I called out as he thrashed about with determination, wobbling awkwardly, pulling the green bologna along the floor.

Looking up to the second tier, I see Maria looking down at me with that I-told-you-so face. I gave her one of those smiles that don't extend to the eyeballs.

It became increasingly difficult for me to ignore the fact that the room was ripe with volcanic laughter. All laughed with gusto at our expense. A polite society would've been more gracious and thoughtfully curbed their enthusiasm. But, no, that would be asking too much from these unsophisticated birdbrains. This is why I hate people.

Some of the girls were rolling on the floor. All were swabbing their eyes. They looked at me with a sort of pity that I didn't appreciate. Even the guard, who paused while making her rounds, was doubled over jerking with spastic merriment.

Seduced by the madness, I fall prey to fits of giggling. The laughter had reached such a fevered pitch that I found myself swept up in the moment. Who among us can resist a good belly laugh? Next thing I know and against my superior judgment, I began howling so hard that I couldn't catch my breath. I nearly lost the grip on my bladder. Crouching down to control the thing, I cut it off at the pass. When I stood to my full stature once more, I found myself facing Hennessy.

It was a nasty shock. Her presence had a sobering effect. The expression buzz kill sprang to mind.

"You know, Doughy, I can't tell if you're reasonably intelligent or a fricken retard. Why do you suppose that is?"

This question caught me off guard. I wasn't sure how to respond. This seemed to be a deceptive question, possibly even rhetorical. Every numbskull knows these abstract queries aren't meant to be answered. I gave her my polite face and safely said nothing. One must never overlook the power of nonverbal communication.

"I suppose you've dug your grave deeper still with this stunt."

"I have until Friday. I've got everything under control." I lied.

"Of course you do. I assume you refer to your last will and testament."

Ignoring this, I excused myself and walked around her. The laughter had stopped and was replaced with serious-matter stillness. The girls, realizing that I was in trouble with Hennessey, looked at me with a great deal of pity.

I drag myself up the stairs and popped into Maria's cell.

"You were right again, Maria, I've made a mess of things. You are forever the voice of reason trying to save me from myself. You tried to tell me but once again, your sound judgment had fallen on deaf and dumb earlobes. When am I ever going to learn?"

"It is what it is," Maria said. "The offer to borrow is still on the table. Better you owe me than Hennessey."

"No, I don't borrow money from friends but thank you.

I sat on Maria's bunk feeling sorry for myself. I hear a voice in my head saying, "I'm not going to cry."

That stupid voice rarely knows what the hell it's talking about.

The fat girl poked her head into the cell.

"Hey, Doughy, she said with labored breath, still winded from the stairs.

"Yes." I said in a heavy tone that matched my heart.

"Are you in trouble with Hennessey?"

"Yes."

"We girls decided to call it even. The show you put on was worth the cost of admission. Use what we gave you to pay Hennessey."

A squeal of delight sprung from my lips. Leaping from the bunk, I gave my new fat friend a hug. I approached the railing and looked down to the bottom floor.

"Thank you, Ladies," I shrill. "I love you all." And I did.

Several women looked up and smiled genially.

I returned to Maria's cell and plopped back down on her bunk. All was right with the world once more. I just knew something good would happen today.

"Hallelujah to a holy twist of fate." I hollered to the ceiling.

"That was nice of them." Maria said.

"Yes, it was. You know, Maria, God doesn't only help those who help themselves; he also helps those who can't help them self."

"Lucky for you that appears to be the case."

FIVE

Maria afforded me the high honor of accompanying her on the second tier as she looked down upon fellow prisoners. She would often stand tall and protective beside me. It made me feel safe.

Today we have our eyes on Marylou. She is our resident chronic undresser and cookie thief. Marylou has snatched a pack of cookies off a table where six girls were playing a hand of poker. Maria and I looked at each other with knowing smiles.

"That girl has some ovaries." Maria says.

"Yeah, Biggens."

The woman Marylou had stolen the cookies from was furious. She plunged forward intending to kill. Marylou had successfully managed to cram all six stale Oreo look-a-likes into her mouth. She was straining to swallow before the expected blow.

Marylou got beat down daily, but these hammerings proved as pointless as a court appointed public defender. It is possible that Marylou had the memory recall of a gold fish. More than likely, she was just another crazy.

I felt Maria's hand touch my forearm. I turned to meet her eyes and with a tilt of her head, she motioned me to follow. I did.

"I read something that kept me awake all last night." Maria said as she walked toward her bottom bunk. She reached for the Bible that was open and laying on a neatly folded blanket.

She was sitting on her bunk when she began to read aloud, "A whorish woman leads a man as an ox to slaughter. The house of an adulterous woman is the way to hell. For she hath cast down many wounded: yea, many strong men have been slain by her. Her house is the way to hell, going down to the chambers of death."

That's from the Book of Proverbs, she said with eyes damp. "I don't know how to be different."

As her eyes filled with tears, I could feel a dull pain in my heart.

Blinking away my own tears, I place my hand on hers and squeezed. I removed the Bible that she had balanced on her lap and carefully dog-eared her page.

I turn to Leviticus and read aloud. "You shall not lie with a male as one lies with a female, it is an abomination." I paused here with crinkled brow feeling the weight of these words.

"It calls Homosexuality an abomination."

My heart gets that sick, heavy feeling.

"I can give up the drugs and stealing. That should take care of the lying." I admit, half talking to Maria, mostly speaking to myself. "But to give up women..." The thought of this made me shudder. "The alternative is to remain single until I die." Then I wonder if this is really so bad. I'm not sure.

I flipped back to the page that I had dog-eared. Leaving it open, I placed the Bible on the small metal table and then sat beside Maria. We both stared vacantly at the gray cement floor.

"Why do we do the things we do?" Maria asked.

"Hard to know, what we can't understand we can make mean anything."

"I just want to be a better person."

"Me too."

"I could use a drink, join me?"

"No thanks," I said.

"Sure? It's a good batch."

"Pretty sure, I have a card game and don't want to jangle my iron constitution."

Maria rolled the eyes.

The truth is that hooch is vile. Her offer, though gracious, practically made me recoil. But one mustn't offend.

Maria went to a small waste bin and removed a shampoo bottle containing the fermented brew.

Hooch is made from bread (for the yeast), fruit, and warm water, which are held in an airtight bag until it becomes alcoholic. In every instance, good batch or not, the creation smells rank. It is the combination of rotten fruit and angry acids. Fermentation takes about a

48

week. At maturity, the adult beverage is strained through a cotton tee shirt. The liquid is then poured into a shampoo bottle so that it may be overtly displayed among our hygiene products.

A Suave Shampoo bottle of hooch sells for four commissary items. It can get you drunk so long as you can keep from vomiting it back up. I tried it once. The tiniest little sip threw me into convulsions of disgust. Consequently, although I'll make hooch you won't catch me drinking up the profits.

+++

While in jail, you'll notice that your dining options dwindle abruptly. Those who place too much importance on food as an adjunct to the perfect life will likely meet with disappointment. If you honor the healing qualities of raw fruits and vegetables, are inclined to fits of nutritional virtue, or believe that a healthy diet and spiritual awareness are fundamentally linked, then this death supporting bill of fare may pose a problem. You can't get a shot of wheatgrass in here.

At 0930 hours inmates are issued a sack brunch which is commonly referred to as a Ladmo bag. The term comes from The Wallace and Ladmo Show, a children's television show produced by and aired in Phoenixville during the mid 1960's. The Ladmo Bag was a prize won by children in a live studio audience. These were small brown paper grocery bags filled with candy, chips, delightful surprises, and sun-drenched hope. These bags were great fun to receive. The ones we get, not so much.

This is why the inmates have their own name for these bags, lame-o. This pronunciation aptly describes its contents. It is rumored to be donated foodstuff that vendor's, in all good conscience, could no longer sell to bona fide human beings.

We're fed twice daily. The next meal is served at 1800 hours. It is a hot meal that we call the salmonella plate. By the time six o'clock rolls around, you're starving and would gladly eat a horse between two mattresses.

Maria empties the contents of the lame-o bag onto the small table in her cell. Out tumbles a green apple complete with its own resident worm colony, greenish bologna trapped in a clear plastic sandwich bag that no one dares to open because it appears to still be breathing, a rock hard roll with somebody's initials carved into it and a packet of decades past its sell-by-date Oreo imposters.

Maria held up the animated lunchmeat.

"Want some?"

"I'm a vegetarian. I'm not opposed to eating a piece of bacon from the contented pig. However, to eat something that still has a pulse is indecent."

Maria flings the pulsating sandwich bag into the trashcan and picked up the cookies. She carefully opens the package and lets the contents tumble onto the table. Six to a package, she twisted each cookie into halves. Using the smooth edge of a short black thin toothed comb, she scraped the white frosting, which looks and tasted more like a communion wafer than sweet creamy goodness, off each cookie half.

I narrow the eyes and put hands on hips. "What in the heck are you up to?"

"Oh, you'll see." she said with a smile that was contagious. I felt the corners of my mouth pull up.

She reached for three tubes of sample sized jail issued mint toothpaste and put a generous portion of paste on each cookie half. Pressing each cookie half back together, she carefully returned each into the packaging. She carried the minty fluoride snacks down stairs and placed them on a lonely tabletop. She then returned to the second tier. We both leaned against the railing in anticipation for A Really Big Show.

As if on cue, Marylou enters the day room. She eyes the cookies like a ravenous tiger stalking a herd of antelope. Within seconds, she had all six cookies in her mouth, wolfing them down like a starving orphan.

Maria and I watched with expectancy, hoping to witness some brutal gag reflex response, or better still, projectile vomiting.

Marylou was completely satisfied without remorse. She knocked a few cookie crumbs off her stripes with the back side of her hand and sauntered back into her cell.

Maria and I felt cheated. We wanted a scene. Baffled we looked at one another.

"What's up with that?" Maria asked.

"Could be you added the missing ingredient. I say we try it.

SIX

I was sitting alone at a table in the day room. Suddenly, Marylou sits across from me accompanied by the scent of sour urine and minty fresh breath. It was a nasty shock. Oh, for God's sake. Lunatics are attracted to me like Drano to a wad of hair.

Marylou is thirty-something, thin medium build with a face that bares a shocking resemblance to Woody Allen. Her right side sags as if stricken by stroke; her right arm dangled lifeless at her side. Her skin is pink flesh white and her hair, cut boy short, is more orange than red. By virtue of the fact that Marylou preferred to be naked, it was easy to conclude that her hair color was authentic. Her whole appearance spelled revolt. Marylou was a woman best seen at a distance, so far away that you can't find her through a telescope.

Seeing Marylou naked was like stepping into an Alfred Hitchcock movie. Despite your best efforts, it was impossible not to look at her when she was in a state of undress. It is similar in the way the eyes are involuntarily drawn to the stump of an amputated leg.

Under normal circumstances, the girls would be kind to one so freakish knowing her life must've been a living hell. These women have seen trouble enough and feel for the unfortunate. However, Marylou steals cookies. All hated her.

I felt Marylou looking down at what I was working on. As was usual, I didn't want to be bothered. I was as unwelcoming as it was possible to be this side of friendly. I keep my head down and my eyes focused on the task. The portrait of concentration, I pretended not to notice her.

"Quadratic formula," Marylou said.

Now she's got my attention.

I look up at her in utter disbelief. Quadratics is to me what a crossword puzzle is to the wordsmith. It is my solitaire. After losing one's self in numerous carefully executed mathematical equations, you're left with a set of solutions that, when plugged into the original equation, provides proof positive that you've gotten it all WRONG. Consequently, the quadratic equation is a metaphor that magically sums up my entire existence.

"Do you know Algebra?" I asked. My eyes are squinty with cynicism.

"Algebra, Calculus, and Trig."

I press my lips into a thin line and make narrow the eyes. I wasn't buying it.

"Really?"

"Yep," she said returning my smile displaying crooked yellow teeth.

"Then perhaps you can tell me, what is pi?"

Crossing my arms at the chest and leaning back, I look at her expectantly.

Marylou inserts a probing index finger into her nostril and digs out a greenish yellow booger. With her thumb and forefinger, she rolls it into a sizable ball. I couldn't help but wonder how Martha Steward might view this variety of table etiquette. Marylou placed the contents of her nose on the underside of the table. I make a mental note to never sit there.

"Pi is the ratio of the circumference to the diameter of a circle, approximately equal to 3.1415926535...to infinity."

I sat stymied. I found myself at a complete loss for words.

"Did you know," Marylou continued, "that Pi is a never-ending, pattern-less succession of numbers. It includes every possible finite sequence, all of the permutations and therefore produces a copy of everything that has ever lived. As a result, there isn't simply one of every person; there are an infinite number of variations of us, each one, one number different. We all lead virtual lives in pi. We're immortal."

I sat immobile and jack-jawed. What a powerful mind, I marveled to myself. She must live virtually on omega 3 fatty acids.

Her answer was well beyond my level of comprehension. This is undeniable proof that she must be right. Why, if I don't understand it, it must be profound. I found myself wondering what that brain of hers must weigh.

What's the deal with her anyway? She's scary smart, noticeably "out there" and has all the natural grace of an orangutan. She's no doubt some accident of chemistry: Schizophrenia, Autism, Idiot savant. Did you see Rain Man?

People with high IQ's are plagued with a mental disorder of one kind or another. In any case, they are typically too smart to be happy.

"I don't understand," I said.

"I'm not talking about your definition of pi, naturally that sailed right over the noggin. No, I mean you're obviously a gifted brainiac yet you risk life and limb to steal cookies. In case you haven't noticed this is not a church social. You know," I said leaning in conspiratorially, "there are women here who could snap your neck like a number two pencil and chalk the effort up as a measly inconvenience. With your swift intelligent mind, surely you must be aware of the fact that you're on everyone's shit list."

"I'm not afraid to die." Marylou said. "So silly really, none of us actually die, we just change form." Chuckling at the thought of it she says, "Nothing and nobody can touch, even in the slightest, the radiant quintessence of who we really are."

"Is that right?"

"Yes it is."

I wasn't sure how to take Marylou.

"The only thing any of us really have is our light," she tells me. "Everything else is temporary, on loan from God: our families, our belongings, these bodies, even this Woody Allen face of mine."

It was as if she had read my mind. I blushed in spite of myself.

"We are all light energy vibration." Marylou explained. "We're psychic energy. Everyone is an actuating, vibrant spiritual being first, last and always. Eventually we all become a ghost of sorts. Get it?"

Marylou eyed the blank slate that was my face.

"Have you heard a thing that I've said?"

She put me on the spot. I see now there are no limits to Marylou's brainpower. She must live chiefly on fish. The next thing you know she'll be expecting me to take an intelligent interest on the subject of orthodox Freudianism. I found myself as absent as a bear in deep winter.

"You're light energy and one day I'm going to be a ghost." I replied as if reciting a lesson verbatim. "What you're saying is outrageous. There I said it."

"Oh, Really," Marylou said in a singsong tone that told me she was too polite to call me a moron.

"So, you think what I'm saying is farfetched do you?"

I answered by way of furrowed brow and a facial expression that radiated confusion. She couldn't have made less sense if she had been speaking in tongues.

Life is rife with questions that befuddle. I'm repeatedly astounded by the tonnage of what I don't understand. My brain has always stood between me and my total understanding of the universe.

Marylou wore the look of defeat. She sighed heavily shaking her head slowly from side to side. For a minute, I thought she might cry. I found myself starting to feel sorry for her. Marylou looked at me with the air of a teacher taking pains with a wayward but promising child. She took a deep breath trying to manage her frustration.

"Let me put it another way."

She pressed on with renewed determination.

I found her to be oddly compelling. Captivated, I lean toward her like a flower toward the sun. If I pay attention, maybe I'll learn something.

"Close your eyes."

I looked at her with suspicion.

"Come on, close your eyes. I'm not going to wipe a booger on you."

I suppose she heard me think that too. With reluctance, I shut one eye and then the other.

"Good, now, take a deep breath, relax, and look toward the center of your forehead."

I breathe in deeply, relaxed and focused on a background field of black and grays.

"Do you see the little flashes of light?"

As I relaxed, I began to notice circles of light that looked like smoke rings. One circle was visible and then it would drift forward and dissipate. Another, than another followed. The billowing light moved in much the same way a cloud floats in perfect rhythm to some greater purpose. As I watched the drifting circles of light, a great stillness arose within me, an unfathomable sense of peace. In that moment, I understood that I was exactly where I was supposed to be and that everything was going to be alright.

"Do you see the light?" Marylou repeated.

"Yes, I see it."

"That's who you are." She said. "That light has been with you all along hidden in plain sight. Contained therein is the truth that will guide you to your highest good, your true-life purpose. Jesus tells us; know the truth and the truth will set you free. The truth to which he points is the truth of who you are. This is not something to believe but to realize. Be strong in the Lord and never give up hope. God has his hand on you, Janie. You're going to do great things."

I was flattered by what seemed to be the greatest encouragement and compliment I've ever received from anyone who wasn't my Mother. I was thrilled and overwhelmed with possibility. Choked up, I felt like I might cry.

"He does? I am?" I managed to squeak out.

With heightened heart rate and a new sense of purpose, I opened my watery eyes, wakey, wakey.

Marylou was gone.

SEVEN

Everything about Angel said bad news. Even her priors had priors. Her stay here would be short, a mere pit stop en route to her final destination, the Arizona State Prison Complex.

Angel is a woman who has been through the fire. What fire doesn't destroy it hardens. She was steeped in a look that said she has seen too much. Bad habit was written on the inside of her arms in the form of track marks, evidence of a lifelong addiction to heroin. She told me she was arrested on charges of counterfeiting. The girls told me she was a hooker.

Rumors and hearsay born out of insufficient information and vivid imaginations take hold in this place like wild fire. I take most of what's said with a grain of salt.

There was something about Angel that tugged on me mysteriously. We were complete opposites in every possible respect. We were, each to the other, a perpetual freak show with no charge for admission. Ours was a pointed illustration of the old adage, opposites attract. My delusional optimism and her sourpuss worldview made us the ideal study of contradictions. I found my attraction to her was much like my former drug habit. What had started as amusement turned obsessive.

Although not attractive by societal standards, Angel behaved as if she was beautiful. It was the secret of her charm. Angel is Hispanic, petite and in her forties with the figure of a fit teenage girl. She has glossy black hair she often wore in a long ponytail, eyebrows that were tweezed into a steep arch that suggested constant astonishment and eye lashes impossibly long and thick.

Her face was a beautiful mask of mistrust. Her posture an elaborate pose to show she didn't give a shit about anything. Angel was a bitch. This made her unpopular with most, but not with me. I found her simply adorable and near perfect. Angel is a wildcard. She's a loose cannon, unmanageable and dangerous. That's hot.

My attraction to Angel was so powerful it felt almost like the onset of illness. When in her presence a strange numbness came over me. My tongue gets knotted and heavy. I can't muster up the courage to simply ask her how she is doing. One wistful look from her and my heart turned liquid.

Angel was a flirt. I remember the first time she gave me one of her smoldering gazes. She was coming down the stairs from the second tier. I was ascending. Her flirtation caught me completely off guard. I became self-conscious. My face felt hot enough to ignite paper.

My heart began to pound uncontrollably as Angel stepped toward me. Her come hither smile had all the effects of a hit of purple microdot and terrific news delivered simultaneously. I clutched the stairs railing to steady my emotions. Nervous, I grinned widely like a chimpanzee and walked clumsily around her stammering some incoherent nonsense. I appeared every bit an imbecile.

I've always been painfully awkward and hopeless when it comes to matters of this sort. I'm typically baffled by another's interest in me. I don't think myself particularly fascinating.

As I headed to my cell, I considered what had just happened. I could feel my eyes were sparkling and I wanted to clap my hands in girlish glee. I felt light headed and giddy. Ah destiny! What dost thou have in store for me? It was turning out to be a glorious day. I found the whole of it exhilarating. I felt like I could fly. This sort of thing is bound to happen I supposed. After all, placing a lesbian in jail is equivalent to housing a canary in a birdseed silo.

The truth is I'd never act on my amorous impulses with Angel or anyone in here. God only knows where they've been. Besides, when it comes to sex I have more hang-ups than a cold-caller peddling used suppositories.

The other thing is that I'm hypersensitive to germs. I see these detainees as an eminent health risk. What with the Hepatitis, a host of treatment resistant flesh eating fungal infections and those diseases indigenous to filthy surroundings, this place is a breeding ground for the next Bubonic plague. Be it real or imagined, I keep myself to myself.

Angel has one good eye, chestnut brown with a trace of jaundice likely due to hepatitis she contracted via dirty needles. Her other eye is a prosthetic. If she moved her head too quickly in any direction the glass appendage meandered independently. But, if she holds her head very still you can hardly tell, sort of. When feeling self-conscious, Angel suspends a cupped hand over the glass-eye making one curious as to what she's trying to conceal. The eye loss was courtesy of a shitty mother.

We were playing a game of Hearts in the dayroom when Angel gave me a glimpse into her childhood. I put my cards down and listened intently.

"I was physically abused by my mother until the age of six." Angel explained. "That's what my father told me. I don't remember most of it."

It was rare for Angel to speak on such personal a matter. I sat across the table from her pleased to be in her company and fully present.

"I do remember the day I lost my eye. My mother hit me in the face with a hot steam iron. 'I hate you. I wish you were never born', my mom's exact words." Angel said sadly.

She was looking down at her fingers, using one hand to massage each finger in its turn. It was a nervous tic of sorts. I'd noticed she did this often.

"I didn't do anything. I tried to be a good little girl."

Angel looked to me with a weary bewilderment. Her good eye was edged with sadness going dark with grief and pain. She appeared suddenly small like an innocent child. I felt a surge of affection for her. I wished desperately that I could make things all better.

"My father stepped in and took me away from my mother." Angel said.

Angel told me that her parents were never married. Her eye went without professional medical attention until she was thirteen. I can't begin to fathom the hell that was her teenage years, let alone her childhood. She came from horrifying beginnings setting the tone for instability. This might explain why she's a mother to eleven children, none of which share the same father. It naturally follows that Angel could keep a panel of psychologists gainfully employed well into the twenty-fifth century.

+++

A guard kindly dropped off the cleaning supplies I had requested and I was mopping my floor. Once a week, I give the place a real good cleaning. I like to wake up to a sanitized environment. Keeping things clean and in order provides the illusion of control. I love my illusions. When I'm finished, I placed the rag, ammonia-cleaning solution and mop into the bucket and carry it downstairs.

"Hey, are you done with that?" One of the girls asked.

"Yep," I said handing over the supplies.

"Thank you."

"You're Welcome."

When I get back to my cell I find Angel sitting on the stool waiting for me. Shaken, I nearly trip over my flip-flop. Catching myself, I greet her with a hello accompanied by an involuntary chimpanzee grin.

Forgoing the customary greeting, Angel said, "I need your help."

"Of course, anything. You seem upset. What's the matter?"

"Do you remember that page-two they hit me with last month?"

Naturally, I remember vividly and in 3-D anything that has to do with Angel. I'm ultra aware of her every nuance much the way a plant will breathe in from the air the substance it needs.

For those not up on the lingo, a page-two is another offense charged against you while you happen to be in the slammer for something else. It is a state of affairs most disagreeable. The same thing happened to me two months ago. I neglected to give you details. I was afraid it might tarnish your elevated opinion of me. It had

60

something to do with a ludicrous allegation that the vehicle I was driving at the time of my arrest had come up stolen. Rather the laughable coincidence as I explained to my accuser. It was just some crazy mix up. I'm expecting an apology any day now.

"You mean the page-two where you sold the VIN-less Jet Ski to some guy who was supposed to take it to Rocky Point, Mexico?" I ask.

"That's the one."

Angel was twisting her fingers. I saw a pinch of pain flitter across her face as she considered the matter.

"Everyone knows vehicle identification plates are a dime a dozen in Mexico." She said through clenched teeth. "Oodles of stolen vehicles pass through that fricken border daily without a hitch. And I get popped for a lousy Jet Ski. It is such crap!"

Angel stopped twisting the fingers long enough to pound a balled up fist into her open palm.

She's so cute. The fire in her singular eye made it sparkle.

"Well, when you put it that way, it does seem rather unfair." I say in my pacifying voice. Her frazzled nerves needed balm.

"You're darn right it's unfair!"

Angel's forehead is crinkled. I feared her head might explode.

"I should've known better than to deal with that retard."

"So you knew the guy?"

"Yes, he's the spineless tweeker who lives across the street from us. I should've had better sense then to deal with that moron." She moaned, chastising herself.

"It is no secret that a tweeker is rarely reliable." I said. "They are known for their extreme paranoia and barefaced dishonesty. I know because I was one. We aren't above stealing your stuff only to help you look for it."

Angel stood staring at me with her one good eye. Without that, other eye she's twice as hard to read. I'm not sure if I said too much or if she wanted to talk and was just waiting her turn.

"So get this," she continues. "The douche bag gets to the border and for some reason they wouldn't let him through."

"I've been to the Mexican border," I said. "Hell, they let everyone through."

"Yeah Right? Odds are that halfwit was riding dirty. I can see him pulling up to the check point with a joint tucked behind his ear." Angel shakes her head in disgust.

"Is he that stupid?"

"He's a complete moron."

"Oh, my, what were you thinking?"

"I was desperate. Do you have any idea what he did?" Angel pauses, looking at me with a mixture of disbelief and challenge.

"I give up, what did he do?"

"He heads back to Phoenixville whining like a bitch and reports the Jet Ski stolen. He paints himself a victim of fraud and is demanding restitution. Who would've thought that birdbrain knew what the word restitution means."

"I'll bet the cops coached him." I mumble.

"Probably, anyway, as you can see, I had no choice but to protect myself."

"Too true, protecting self is the prudent course of action, but how do you mean?"

"Two weeks ago I gave Loretta twenty-five dollars worth of commissary in payment for her services."

"Her services you say?"

"Yes, she sends her goons out to terrorize and if need be mutilate "would be" plaintiffs.

"Well then, problem solved."

"That was what I thought until I called my daughter. I asked her if doofus across the street was still walking upright. She said all his limbs were still intact."

"Uh-oh."

"Uh-oh is right. That nincompoop should be in a wheelchair, on a respirator, or wearing a colostomy bag by now. I go to court for this bullshit in three days."

"That will be here before we know it."

"That's why Loretta needs to fulfill her end of our contract, pronto."

Angel's eye darkened, she took in a deep breath, and then like a crazy person she kicked at the air.

"You seem to be in a bit of a pickle. What do you intend to do about it?"

"The way I see it Loretta needs a wakeup call. If she wasn't such an Amazon I'd take care of the matter myself, but as it stands I'm going to need your help."

"The woman is vast and imposing." I pointed out in alarm.

At first glance, the term gargantuan springs to mind. You might say Loretta is solid proof, once and for all, that we're related to the apes.

"You aren't suggesting that I assist in manhandling that colossus, are you?"

"You only need to hold her down. I'll take care of the rest."

I allowed a few moments to pass giving her time to change her mind. She looked at me expectantly. It must be my turn.

"So, forgive, forget, and vengeance is mine said the Lord, isn't something you wish to mull over?"

I braced myself for the nervous prattle that always takes over when I'm not sure what to say.

"Did you know that unforgiveness is the leading cause of cancer?" Here I pause, then that inner something pitches me into automatic. "This is Stanford University research. I didn't make that up. I know you hate when I bring up the Bible, but it says that it is our duty to forgive even until seventy and seven times."

Angel furrowed the brow and gave me a look as if she was an Eskimo and I was trying to sell her a freezer. I can't help but notice that logical reason is often wasted on her. She really is very cute but she has heart leather like a turtle has a shell. Not a thing one can soften with sound advice.

"Okay," I said changing the approach.

"My holding Loretta down can be likened to stopping a charging rhinoceros with a dirty look. I'm not a violent woman, Angel. Harmonious monotony is all I strive for. Besides, I have a great respect for all living things. I'm one of those people who carry bugs outside so I don't have to kill them."

"You do?" Angel said pulling a face.

"Yes, I do." I said a little defensively. "You know, one time I broke into a pet store to free the parakeets. I see now it was an idea way before its time. Zoos are full. Prisons are filled to bursting. We live in a society that dearly loves to control by cages.

"You got that right."

"The point I'm trying to make is that I wouldn't harm a fly. This is truer than ever when said fly happens to be the size of Magilla Gorilla."

"Well, I didn't have you pegged for a fighter." Angel said.

She wasn't polite enough to hide her disappointment.

"You would be correct. Besides, I like Loretta."

Angel pressed together the lips and scoffs.

It was hard not to like Loretta. She had a voice that was forever brimming with the possibility of laughter. Sure she was an Amazon but more the gentle giant. She had a face that was easy to look at, almost pretty despite a cleft lip. The top lip split just to the right exposing a half-inch of a front incisor giving the illusion that she was sneering. But of course, she wasn't. Hers was a timid, almost bashful nature. When engaging in conversation, Loretta routinely held a hand in front of her defective mouth in what seemed to be intended as a courtesy and felt a lot like a request for forgiveness. A gesture she learned early and practiced all her life. I often felt the urge to hug her and tell her it didn't matter. But of course, it did matter. It mattered to her.

"I'm certain that Loretta is doing everything she can." I said. "She mentioned something about a lack of cooperation on the part of her peeps on the outs."

"That's her problem. She should've thought about that before she took my money."

"You make a good point."

"What about Maria, do you think she'd help? Maybe you can talk to her."

"Maria?" I stammer. "Well, you should know, Angel, I'm an enormous fan of yours. However, Maria dislikes you in the extreme."

Angels face darkened.

"Screw her!"

"What about Sam?" I offer. "I noticed she drools when in your company. You need only flash that winning smile and she'll be at your beck and call."

Angel cringed making the face of one who accidently swallowed a fly. The mere mention of Sam's name made any civilized person visibly ill.

"I was hoping it would not have to come to that."

"And for good reason," I sympathize. "Sam isn't one I would wish to be obligated to for any reason what so ever. Perhaps I can help." I said compelled by some ridiculous need.

"I can serve as lookout while you and Sam box Loretta's ears. I'm afraid that's all I'm good for."

"That will due. Be downstairs in an hour."

With that Angel turned and she was gone.

Holy Mackerel, I'll say one thing for Angel, once the need for a skirmish presents itself she forges ahead with an energy and determination that demands respect.

The instant Angel exited, remorse entered. I got that sick feeling in my belly. I sat on my bunk with vacant eyes fixed on nothing in particular. Now what have I gotten myself into? This sort of retaliation often turns out badly. I really should learn to shut my mouth. It is a simple matter. I just say nothing at all. BUT NO, I can't do that. I was overcome with a sense of dread. Why must I be such a dumbass?

Growing tired of my pity party, I walked to the sink and splashed my face with water. The stomach churning resumed. Anguish hung over me like a storm cloud.

To ease the tension I decided to see Glenda. Glenda is a soothsayer. The spirits line up in droves to chew the fat with her. She had knowledge of profound and occult matters beyond the scope of ordinary mortals. The overly religious or academic might pooh-pooh her mystic endowments but I find her services vital.

Grabbing my brown paper bag of commissary, I removed a coke and Hersey bar with almonds. This was the fee Glenda charged for a reading. I made sure to order these items each month for occasions such as this. Glenda was tapped into nether worldly things and was able to see future events in Technicolor. I need to know if she saw the spilling of my red blood any time in the extreme near future.

While descending the stairs, I sent a telepathic message giving Glenda a heads-up that I was on my way. I gave a courtesy tap on the door and barged right in. Glenda was reclined on her bunk, hands laced together behind her head.

"Oh hi, Janie, I wasn't expecting you."

"Oh." I was feeling a little let down.

"I need a reading."

I placed the coke and candy bar on her table. Glenda's eyes light up. She sprang up and grinned.

Waving a hand to the chair she said, "Please, sit."

Glenda reaches under her blanket and retrieves a pack of standard playing cards. Since I was sitting on the only chair, Glenda stood. Cracking the seal on the soda top, she takes a life-restoring sip and sighs pleasantly. She tapped the cards on the table then shuffles and cuts, cuts again, and reshuffles then places the cards on the table.

"Cut them." She said.

As I did my part, she adopted an ghostly tone of voice while waving her arms back and forth.

"Is there anybody there? Do you wish to communicate with anyone in this room?"

Glenda puts a finger to her temple to suggest deliberation, stares crazy eyed at the ceiling to hint at the awe-inspiring nature of what was happening, and moans softly to point out how daunting a task this was. Glenda was the real deal.

"Come forth, reveal yourselves old spirits, come, and deliver thine message."

I was tempted to give the table a kick to see how she would react, but then I remember my true purpose for this visit.

"Glenda, I hate to interrupt, but I'm not here to speak with my dead relatives. Not this time. I just need to know if you see me being bludgeoned to death this afternoon."

"Well, why didn't you say so?"

She picked up the deck of cards.

"If you need a quick answer to your question a single card can give an overall impression about your immediate problem."

She holds out the fanned deck. I picked a card and handed it to her. Glenda looked at the card then looked at me.

"Nope, you won't be dying today."

Relieved, I thank Glenda then went back to my cell for a quick healing meditation.

When it was time, I calmly rose from my bunk. I point myself to the open door and head toward it. Even though I wasn't going to die, I was still a little nervous.

When I stepped out of my cell, I saw her. Maria was standing in the thoroughfare, hands on hips, her face a portrait of dissatisfaction. She was looking directly at me. Uh-oh, the sight of her stopped me dead in my tracks. We both stood still drinking each other in. Shit, she knows. Maria walks toward me with the air of a school principle burdened with an unpleasant task. I swallowed hard and put on my happy face.

"Don't you look lovely this fine morning, Maria, my goodness, have you lost weight?"

"Cut the crap, Doughy, where are you going?" It is never a good sign when she uses my last name.

"Nowhere."

I was twisting my knitted hands. I must've picked this up from Angel.

"Look," Maria said wearing her tax auditor face. "I don't want you getting involved in Angel's fresh new disaster."

"I'm just playing lookout."

Maria gave me a look that smacked of disapproval. "It's a real bad idea. Word gets out that you played any part of this and you'll go down with them."

"I know, I know. I should've never volunteered. When I get around Angel, I seem to lose my grip on reality. Everyone knows love turns smart people stupid. The thing is I gave her my word."

Maria sighs deeply.

"Oh for God's sake." She says which was followed by something in Spanish that I couldn't make out. Now she's just standing in front of me, arms crossed, head tilted to the ceiling, eyes closed. She recovers from this position nodding gravely.

"I'll come with you."

"You will? I was scared to death. Could you tell? I've never been a lookout before. I wanted to help and I thought I could handle it."

"Well you can't and you won't do it again."

"Okay, I won't, I promise."

When Maria and I reached the bottom floor, we saw Sam and Angel preparing to enter Loretta's cell. A simple nod was all we needed to signal zero hour. Maria and I took our position a few feet in front of Loretta's now closed cell door.

While providing lookout services, we did a courtesy block for Maureen who was crouched in front of the AC outlet. I stood there observing Maureen's rather MacGyver-esque method of lighting up her cigarette. A trick done through the magical properties of state issued pencil leads. These pencils are short with no eraser like the ones they give out at a golf course or bowling alley. Gnawing, chewing, and ripping away the wood portion of the pencil can remove the lead.

I watched as two pencil leads are inserted into the wall receptacle in the same manner you might insert a plug. Now Maureen has two leads protruding out, side-by-side, but not touching. The third pencil lead is the charm. She takes a narrow strip of toilet paper and wraps it tightly about fifteen times around the center of lead three. She then carefully drops number three lead onto the protruding leads. The placement of lead three closes the circuit sending a surge of alternating current coursing through lead three. This causes sparks that ignite the toilet paper that quickly becomes a flame. It's a thing of beauty. On occasion, this stunt will trip the main breaker, but Maureen is no amateur. When her rollie is lit, she cups the smoke and beelines it to the steamy open bay showers. The steam is meant to mask the smell. Maybe it does a little but I can always smell it.

There was little danger of a guard entering the pod as their movements are as surely timed as the planets and their courses. They walk their rounds every hour then retreat back to the bubble to do paperwork and whatnot. With a cell door closed, the guards can see nothing. Should they suspect suspicious behavior they will listen in on a live audio feed. There are cameras in the dayroom.

Inmate closed door powwows occur a couple times weekly and serve as a means of settling differences. Not every intervention comes to blows and I'm hoping this one won't either. Five minutes pass before Sam and Angel emerge from the cell unruffled. Loretta follows visibly shaken but not stirred. Her look was pale and tragic like one who had narrowly avoided a fatal car crash. Truth always forces its way into the rational mind. Loretta knows that she must make good on their agreement or there will be hell to pay.

EIGHT

Let's all have our period! Menstrual cycles are contagious adding a hint of mystery to our misfortune. It is the period just before "Aunt Blood" is in town when sense and sensibilities are compromised. Foul moods facilitate rising tension that produces a palpable agitation. Tempers heat up faster than a junkie's spoon. Toss in a full moon and these ladies are going for the jugular at the slightest provocation. Where fighting is concerned, this place is better than Pay-per-View. The adage "fights like a girl" takes on a whole new meaning.

The composition of any good upheaval requires estrogen. In this sea of toxic hormones, we seldom got through the morning without a hysterical outburst of some kind. Character assassinations and venomous racial slurs are as commonplace here as diarrhea is to Mexican ice cubes.

I was lying on my bunk mesmerized by the floating specks that seem to be riding on the surface of my retina. I wondered if this was normal or a warning sign that my eyeballs were in decline. My mind toyed with this dreadful prospect and then ranged idly over other subject matter. I thought of love and women, the immortality of the spirit, and the deplorable speed at which an eight ball of crystal meth disappears. That's when a down stairs disturbance fouled my concentration. I decided to see what was causing the hullabaloo.

I poured myself out of the top bunk and headed toward my open cell door. Before I could get a second foot outside the exit, Maria grabbed my arm.

"What's up, My Sister?" I say.

"I don't want you getting mixed up in this." She gives the arm a yank.

"Ouch. Careful with the merchandise, I'm a delicate lotus petal."

"Sorry."

She let go of my bicep.

"What's going on?"

Maria looked over the railing to the bottom floor. I follow suit. I see Angel arguing with four very pissed off women.

"Angel snitched on Loretta," Maria said. "She told the guard that Loretta was trading meds for commissary."

"Holy shit."

Maria gave me a sad frown.

"Yep, the guards already hauled Loretta off to the hole. Those girls in a huddle are Loretta's customers. Their drug supply has been cutoff and now they are fit to be tied."

"Uh-oh. This is definitely not good. Are you sure Angel snitched? I know she was angry at Loretta, but she isn't an idiot."

Maria gave me a look as if to suggest otherwise.

"What could she have been thinking? Snitching is the kind of thing people get dead over. Angel knows better than that."

"Well," Maria said, "you can lead a whore to water but you can't make her think."

I raised the brow in offense.

"Well, I just won't believe it! And besides, Angel isn't a whore. She's an unlicensed massage therapist."

I gave Maria a look that dared her to disagree.

"Oh sure. It's the happy endings that keep her customers coming back."

"You're talking perfect nonsense. Not that it matters anyway. Angel is a very clever girl. I'm certain that she's good at whatever she puts her mind to."

"You mean mouth."

Holy Mackerel, defending Angel is a fulltime job. It'd be easier to defend pedophilia. Poor thing is so misunderstood.

"When Angel laughs," I begin to recite from memory, "the skies are blue, all the joyful cows go moo. A squirrel in the garden, the children sing and joy is a part of everything.

When Angel laughs... When Angel cries, When Angel cries..."

"What in God's name are you going on about?" Maria said crinkling the forehead as if the sound of my voice was like nails on a chalkboard.

"It is a poem. I wrote it for Angel last night. Do you think the cow thing is too much? Maybe you should hear more?"

"NO."

Now she looks like she just swallowed a bad oyster.

"No?"

"No!"

"Well I just thought…"

"Well you thought wrong!"

"Fine."

I was more than a little hurt. There is good stuff in Maria. Her heart is always in the right place just aching for your difficulties. When it comes to giving advice Maria comes right to the heart of the matter. Unlike me, whose sound advice is ninety-nine percent sound. All of which can be classified as noise pollution.

Despite all of Maria's redeeming qualities, I feel a need to lodge a nagging complaint. She has an uncanny way of making me look like damaged goods. With one cutting observation, she can make a cleverly camouflaged character flaw of mine as obvious as an elephant sandwich. I've never been a big fan of blunt observations, unless I was making it. I mean to say, sure I want people to be honest with me but not to my face!

Avoiding further insult, I peeked over the railing to size up the situation.

"It's zero hour. I'm going in."

"Suit yourself."

Maria wore the look of exasperation. She took in great amounts of air, followed by a long, weighty sigh.

"I can't have your back on this one."

"Fine!"

Crossing myself for protection, I head toward the stairs.

+++

Reaching the bottom tier, I feel a meaty paw on my shoulder.
I cringe.

"Jesus, Sam! You know I don't like to be touched!"

Raising both beefy ham hands in the air apologetically, Sam took a step back. She gave me a big toothy grin to let me know she was the one for me.

I return the smile to let her know that I thought she should take some sheep shears to that upper lip, but I don't think my message was conveyed. There was a carpet sample beneath her beak. It looked, for all the world to see, like a patch of poorly assigned pubic hair.

"I'm sorry, Sugar Plum."

Sam spoke with a slowness of speech suggestive of some primitive form of inbreeding. You know the kind where your Paw just happens to also be your Grand Pappy who just happens to be livestock.

Sam told me that her name isn't short for anything. It was a matter of mistaken identity at birth. Her frazzled mother had twelve children in thirteen years. Sam was the twelfth. When Sam was born, her Mom couldn't decide her sex.

"I was about two years old when Ma finally figured out what was what. By that time she was already used to the name and so she said, screw it."

Sam is a woman who doesn't know the meaning of drop dead or go to hell. One cell short of a brain, Sam is one of nature's greatest blunders. Her ignorance is inexhaustible and appalling. Sam couldn't predict the time one hour from now. She's a flatulent fool of indeterminable gender that invited both curiosity and mental confusion.

Sam is a perfect size sixteen with a stump shape, a no-nonsense buzz cut, and shoulders that would grace an ox. Like a bad wig, Sam is a disturbing element. Her presence leaves one with nausea you could neither account for nor dismiss. Everything about her offended me. A sentiment compounded by the blunt sexual relish with which she inspected my breast as she spoke. This vulgar habit alone makes her a threat to public decency.

"Why don't you go back to your cell and read a book, Sam?"

"I ain't read no book in..."

Here she pauses with crumpled brow. It was painful to observe Sam's brain trying to function.

73

"Why it's been thirty years I reckon."

Wearing the look of one who smells an escape of sewer gas, Sam added, "I hate to read."

"Really, you can barely tell."

"I know you like me." Sam said with an eerie sureness.

A shudder ran down my frame. I was wondering what I might've done to lead her to this conclusion.

"No. I don't."

I pulled a face and took a step back.

"I'm predicting a closed casket funeral for your girl tomorrow. I think you and me will make a right nice pair."

Sam is grinning hugely, like a three year old, as if what she just said was high wit.

"I wouldn't touch you with a pair of tongs at the end of a ten foot pole."

"Whatever you say, Sweet Tits."

Sam is looking at my chest with rather piggy eyes.

"I sure would like to help you with that problem you have with being touched."

Feeling a wave of nausea, I clench the teeth. I glare. Nuisances like Sam shouldn't be encouraged. I couldn't help myself.

"I'd rather masturbate with a hook."

"I don't reckon I like your attitude, Little Missy."

"I don't have an attitude. You're just an asshole."

Having my fill, I hastily made my way around her.

I head toward Angel who was leaning semi reclined, her butt against a table, legs crossed at the ankles, and hands gripping the table edge like it was her only friend. The four angry inmates were standing in a huddle, no doubt drawling straws. Angel's fate was already decided. It is cut and dried, street thug simplicity. Either you live or not.

As I approached Angel, I smiled warmly but she didn't notice. She had the look of an animal that sensed a trap. When she became aware of my presence, she deliberately swiveled her singular eye away, freed one hand from the table, and made a production of examining her fingernails. I slide in beside her. With our arms touching, I could feel the tension in her body.

"Is it true?" I asked.

Angel said nothing. Deep in concentration, she forced a cuticle up with her thumbnail. I heard in her silence absolute confirmation.

"Are you okay?"

Even as I asked the question the absurdity of it struck me. There we remained in an awkward silence. It was like trying to make small talk with someone whose next seat was slated to be an electric chair. I can't remember the last time I felt this uncomfortable.

The short straw stepped toward us.

"Move along, Janie, this got nutten to do with you."

She was right. I squeezed Angel's bicep reassuringly and stepped aside. What happened next happened fast.

With the heel of her right hand, Angel delivered an upper cut to short straw's nose. Blood streamed from her nostrils like a fully open faucet. The girl's eyes rolled up until only the whites shown and her legs twisted out from under her. The poor thing dropped like a sack of potatoes. She hit the concrete floor so hard that you could hear the sound of her skull cracking. The orgy of violence was mesmerizing.

Confounded, the onlooker's stood paralyzed with mouths wide open. They all wore the expression of one who had just discovered that they were fondling a tarantula.

I basked in the glow of their shock. The tension in the air was delectable. That's my girl. Elated, I wanted to cheer. What I'd give right now for a set of pompoms and the ability to do the splits.

Reminding myself that few seem to share in my passion, it's best to talk myself down off this pink cloud. Non-reaction on my part required great effort.

Short straw was lying senseless on the floor. It should've been over but it wasn't. She became the recipient of decades of repressed rage and hostility. Angel continued to whale on her listless body. She delivered each lethal thrust with a zealous light in her eyes like an Evangelical pounding the lectern. She didn't seem to tire. She showed no sign of stopping. There was unmistakable triumph and satisfaction in her demeanor.

Short straw began to take on the appearance of a corpse rather than the preferred, trauma victim. I found myself wishing that she hadn't been nice to me. I was beginning to feel sorry for her. I stepped in as a token response.

"You can stop now, Sweetheart. You know how daunting those pesky manslaughter charges can be."

Ignoring me, Angel began kicking the girl in the face.

The security alarm bellowed and four armed guards stormed into the pod. Medics with a stretcher followed. The guards threw my little princess to the wall and cuffed her.

I tried to explain to the officers that she was a victim of circumstances, but they said according to the video, "she was no victim."

"Darn those bastard cameras!"

The officer shot me a look that said I was one outburst away from meeting Mister Tazor.

I decided to shut my mouth.

The pitiable truth is if Angel had dowsed every inmate with gasoline and set them on fire with a blowtorch, I could justify her actions. Then too, what can't be settled by mere words can often be accomplished with a flamethrower.

I saw Angel standing cuffed outside the ward. I felt my heart give a terrible little twist. I knew it would be the last time I'd see her.

Like a basketball referee calling a traveling violation, Angel rolled one fisted hand in a circular motion around the other. She mouthed the words, "rollup my stuff".

I nodded to Angel and headed to her cell. Upon entering, I discover bottom feeders had beaten me to it. The frenzy I witnessed reminded me of a mob fight I saw at Wal-Mart, one Black Friday, over the last Xbox 360. Shooing away the parasites, I wrapped what remained in a bed sheet and placed it on a table in the dayroom. Only county issued items remained. Her favorite paperbacks and anything commissary was pilfered. She has so little. Why couldn't they just keep their mitts off her few meager comforts? I hate them! I wanted to punch every one of them right in the face. And I would've if I hadn't been certain that they would kill me. I looked through the quadruple paned glass once more. Angel was gone.

Despondent, I navigated the stairs. I moved with an aura of resignation as if I were forcing myself to put one foot in front of the other. I made my way to my assigned bunk. My gloom filled the cell like a fog. My heart was so heavy that it hurt. I sat on my bunk idly toying with a length of string I had pulled out of my jail issued nightshirt.

These ugly gray cotton garments are stitched together with a string of a heavier thread count making it ideal for plucking the eyebrows. I had spent many hours in practice by removing leg hairs. Because there are no mirrors eyebrow threading is a service we do for one another. Some exchange for canteen items. I don't charge if you're cute. I won't do it if you're not. Does this make me shallow?

Maria entered the cell where I sat dull eyed and listless. It is amazing how she always turns up at the crucial moment like the Army Reserves.

"Hey" she said.

"Hey."

"You okay?"

I shrug.

Maria hopped up, sat beside me, and placed an arm around my shoulders.

"I know your heart is broken." Maria said, giving my shoulder a squeeze.

I hate it when I have difficult emotions under wraps and someone comes along extending sympathy and kindness. It always brings to light just how pathetic I must look. The moment Maria put an arm around my shoulder, I knew things were going to get ugly. My lip turned down like a baby and the next thing I know it is Niagara Falls.

"I don't want to talk about that." I manage to eke out.

"No?"

"No, the past is dead. Let's say no more about it."

"Okay."

"I've been injured to the deepest recesses of my soul, but what's done is done. That's the end of it."

"That's fine."

"Just ignore it. Forget it ever happened." I lament.

"We can do that."

"That was some fight don't you think?" I say blinking away tears.

"Impressive. Angel throws a mean right uppercut."

"Don't say the name! Do you think I'm made of marble?"

"Sorry."

"And do you want to know what the worst of it is?"

I slap the mattress hard.

"What's the worst of it?

"I didn't put a single cent on that fight. What could I have been thinking? That fight was a goldmine just waiting to line my pockets with joy."

I slapped the mattress again even harder.

"How could I be so stupid?"

"You did put money on that fight." Maria said.

"I did?"

"That's correct."

Maria grinned widely displaying a lovely set of even pearly whites.

I felt my spirits begin to lift sharply.

"Spill it and don't leave out the slightest detail."

"Eight entered the pool, ten dollars to play."

"Short-straw was the favorite to win, right?" I say with buoyancy rising. "The consensus of opinion was that Angel didn't have a chance in hell?"

"You got it."

"But YOU, in your infinite wisdom, put it all on Angel."

"Right again."

"The pots at eighty dollars with two winners, you and I. Forty each, minus ten percent admin fees to Hennessey, why that's thirty-six bucks a piece."

I looked at Maria sheepishly, "what do I owe you."

Maria raised a restrictive hand.

A jubilant squeal escaped from my lips. "You're Brilliant! I Love you! You saved my life! The voices of one hundred Angels could not express my gratitude. I shall never grow tired of boasting on your behalf. Do you realize this gets me out of the red?"

"How deep did you dig yourself in this time?"

"Well," I said beginning to feel a little ashamed. "I owe Hennessy twelve and then there was that "FERTIE EXTRAVAGANZA" thing that set me back another fifteen."

"I thought the girls let you keep that."

"Yeah, but I managed to mismanage that windfall."

Maria shook her head in disapproval.

"You have a gambling problem."

"I don't think so." I said defensively.

"I can't see how all the betting you do doesn't conflict with your spiritual endeavors."

Maria won't let up.

I was obliged to yield to this point.

"In this environment the smart money says gambling needs the attention."

My arms are crossed, eyes narrowed.

"Of course, I know gambling is wrong. Definitely not the thing to develop one's higher self and you can forget about the pearly gates." I say, softening to this reality.

"Do you think I like being a hypocrite, Maria? Nobody does. It is just too hard to stay faithful to all virtue. Everyone believes in virtue but who among us is virtuous?"

"It does seem we all struggle to be good people in an imperfect world." Maria said.

"That's what I'm trying to say!"

Finally, I'm feeling vindicated.

"Moral principle is a life path for the martyr and saint whose minds are like a still pond. These people sleep on beds of nails when they aren't walking on broken glass. They are sinless wonders just bursting through the pores with restraint and integrity. I know a thing or two about integrity and I can assure you, I don't have any. Sure, gambling is

79

a habit that leads me running from the promise land. However, the fact is there are so few vices that I can exercise in this place, I feel oddly entitled."

"Oddly disemboweled is what you'll be if you don't watch your P's and Q's. From now on you'll run your harebrained schemes past me before making shares available to the general public."

I generally like to take a mature attitude toward things. Unfortunately, Maria makes this impossible. I only put up with her out of deference to her quick intelligence and abundant goodness.

"Well, Maria, just say whatever is on your mind. Don't let my fragile, highly susceptible nature keep you from yielding that Ginsu knife. It is only a matter of time before this place makes me as hard as a slab of granite. There is certainly no reason why you shouldn't aid and abet my stony development."

"Quit being a baby."

Finding this last comment troubling, I gave her a dismissive sniff. Once again, Maria insists on taking the thing one sentence too far. She knows that I hate when she says that. Our eyes met and I dished out a full serving of my acid glare. A half second passed, we were frozen in time. Then Maria smirks. It seemed keeping a straight face required great effort on her part. I found myself contemplating her with great annoyance.

"I can take care of myself." I blurted out. "This isn't my first day at the rodeo you know. Genius can't be burdened by maturity."

I was becoming a churning mass of non-sequiturs.

"And another thing," I whimper. "I take offense to the word harebrained."

I brooded for a long moment in silence then I acquiesce.

"I freely admit that the last 'sure thing' I had conjured up threw me under the bus."

"You mean the mouse in a cup scheme?"

"Go ahead, make fun. I suppose I need these kinds of trials to make me more spiritual. It's frightfully difficult to become enlightened while in this social leper colony surrounded on all sides by jackasses."

"Too true," Maria said. "I'd love to love my neighbor, but too many insist on making this a complete impossibility."

I nodded in agreement.

"It is simply too hard to love someone when you desperately want to chop them into tiny bits so that they may rest in pieces."

"Rest in pieces." I repeat and giggle.

"You know," I said reflectively. "Fertie is the most tranquil and unimposing of God's creatures. I turned him into a one-trick pony for my own personal gain."

I cringe at the thought of this.

"I'm a selfish person. I should be ashamed of myself."

"Look!" Maria said. "There he is."

I looked down at the floor to see a mouse entering the cell.

"That isn't Fertie, he is very handsome. That mouse is rather average."

The mouse looked up at us and seemed to ask, "Got any of that green bologna?" In unison, Maria and I nodded gravely in the negative.

Seeming to say "thanks anyway", the little fellow did an about-face and scurried to the next cell to try his luck there.

"They all look the same to me." Maria said.

"I can't believe you just said that."

+++

When Maria was released, I missed her terribly. She had written me a month later. She landed a job as a hotel receptionist. She decided to get legit for the sake of her boys. She had always said she loved her son's more than she hated herself.

It seemed to me that a prostitute working in a hotel could be likened to a recovering alcoholic taking a job as a bartender. Keeping this view to myself, I sent a letter back just saturated with encouragement. I had developed an enormous respect and admiration for Maria. I was impressed by many things about her but mostly by her kindness. The kind that comes from learning hard lessons well. The kind fills me with a sense of admiration. I felt privileged that Maria saw fit to befriend and confide in me.

NINE

Grace is twenty-two and the glamour of youth was around her. She has large brown eyes like a Jersey cow, shoulder length auburn hair, and almond skin. She had undeniable appeal. Grace wasn't a woman of swift intelligence, more sweet than smart.

First impression might lead one to believe that on the outs, Grace routinely answered the door in short shorts and a "spank me" tee shirt.

Grace was wholly preoccupied with sex. Whenever a male officer was on duty, which was seldom, Grace would strip down to nothing and try to entice the guard into her lair. When she was being carted off to solitary confinement we all knew why.

Grace would regularly meander into my cell, walk up to where I sat on the top bunk with my legs dangling, and stare directly into my crotch, like she had plans for it. She would then look up, our eyes would meet, and with a wicked smile and in a voice suitably lewd she would say, "I love you, Janie."

Grace was more seductive than smack. Sex appeal rose from her like a cloud of steam. It took everything I had to keep myself from committing the unthinkable. The crotch gaze I could withstand. However, everyone knows the phrase "I Love you" is a lesbian mating call that instantaneously triggers thoughts of U-Haul rental and long-term domestic partnership.

Fortunately, no alcohol was involved or things could have gotten ugly. I could rarely resist meeting her scandalous grin with the same despite the fact that I'm twice her age and mindful of her inferior mental endowment. As I drift into the various thoughts of what I'd like to do to her in private, I'm jolted out of my musing by the feel of her tugging on my pants in a southerly direction. I make her stop.

Women who chase after a woman twice their age suffer from maternal depravation. I call it "Love me Mommy" disorder. When the woman in pursuit is hot, it is flattering. When she isn't, it's annoying. Telling her that you don't love her back and the stalking has to stop only makes her want you MORE. I speak with a staggering degree of authority on this matter and have had numerous restraining orders filed against me to prove it.

On any given day, Grace rarely spoke more than ten words. So, when she told me her story, I felt privileged and listened intently. Hers was a tale that could drag compassion out of a brick. She explained her experience as one might describe details of the latest blockbuster, random highlights, more factual than personal, and meaning nothing. I wanted to tell her that I knew what such a story felt like.

Grace was in the third grade when she came home from school to find her mom swinging from a noose made of extension cord. Her mother hung herself in the living room of the doublewide they called home.

"I put my school books on the kitchen table then took a nap just underneath moms dangling feet." Grace said. "When I woke up I did my homework."

Grace explained that they lived real close to a freeway over pass and whenever the large semi-trucks went by, "the trailer shook and mommy swung a little like she wanted to walk."

Grace always slept with her mom unless mom's newest boyfriend was staying over. Then she would sleep on the couch.

"Sometimes I would sleep with Earl. He made me give him head."

Grace spoke in a tone one might use when asking you to pass the salt. Her lack of emotion was spooky. I was finding it difficult to regret her mommy's demise.

"Two days or two weeks later," Grace said, not sure which, "when the trailer park lady came by for the rent, she peeked in and saw my mom hanging there. I was sleeping underneath."

I was astounded. I've only heard of this sort of thing happening in books. Not to real, people. Not to anyone I know. It could be this sort of thing happens all the time. Maybe I just haven't been paying attention.

"Child Protective Services swooped in to save the day," Grace said. "They dropped me off to live with my Uncle Jake. Uncle Jake liked little girls too."

"Oh my God, that's terrible." I said with a face that crumbled.

Grace shrugs as if to say, 'not so much.'

Her story was upsetting. I felt the tears coming. The girls in here are mostly tearless. When the shedding begins, they are often caught off guard. Tears make some people uncomfortable.

Grace remained unruffled. I was noticeably shaken. Although, I willed it to stay, a tear slipped out. I leaned forward to give Grace a hug. She promptly pushed me away and with melancholy seen-to-much eyes she said, "I can take care of myself. I've had a lot of practice."

"So I figured."

I went back in for the hug. This time she let me. Not because she needed it, but because she understood that I did.

+++

There is nothing like a hand of poker to whisk away the doldrums and invoke the spirit of possibility. Cards are serious business around here.

There is only one person in the card playing circuit that I'd call a friend. This would be my partner, Keisha. She was assigned to this ward in answer to my prayers.

The women we play against would steal their mother's retirement funds and the mattress it was under. We all regard each other with a mixture of mutual coldness and mistrust deriving from our respective situations.

Whenever cards are played there is always an opening for cheats. There is however, a difference between a card shark and a card cheat. A shark is definitely a cheat but a cheat isn't automatically a shark. Keisha is a shark. This woman makes her own luck. She's a strategist, an expert in the art of cheating. The average blockhead doesn't stand a chance against her. Comparing a common cheat to Keisha is to compare shoplifting to the Enron Scandal.

I too could be a poker Goddess if it were not for my face. Whatever I'm thinking shows up on my mug like the trumpeting announcement over a PA system. It happens in an instant. Not a thing that can be controlled. It needs to be fixed. It's a liability.

My poker skills fall within the range of unfortunate too largely embarrassing. Where I excel is in finding a good partner. I do understand the fundamentals of the game. How to make the dealer serve up four Aces and a King is where I am stuck. This isn't to say that I don't have a strategy. I most certainly do. When the cards are dealt to me, I pick them up and gaze intently at them while simultaneously -- and here is the nub of the thing -- pray to the Gods for favor.

Keisha is a black woman of indeterminable age. She's shrewd and classic, an old soul. Keisha is a thin, determined woman with a permanent poker face. She has a way of looking resilient and searchingly at people, which inspires fear. Her eyes are penetrating with the simple directness of a child's. One can't meet them easily. Keisha could do more with the raising of an eyebrow then Moses could do with the Ten Commandments.

The good news is I don't have to be a Cracker Jack card player. I just need to do what Keisha tells me to do. I leave the dealing from the bottom, deck stacking, miss deals, and ambiguous manipulations to her. My job is to cause a distraction. I need only watch for subtle clues and then behave like a well-trained seal.

+++

The game in progress is moving along at a leisurely pace. I notice Keisha is holding her cards with four fingers facing me. This tells me that I need to count clockwise to the fourth person at the table and distract them. Keisha typically holds her cards with a thumb and horizontal forefinger. In this position, I'm to do nothing.

85

There are six at the table. We're each sitting directly across from our partner. Counting clockwise to the fourth person, my eyes fall on Barb. She is sitting to the left of Keisha.

I was preparing myself to slip into suck-up mode. Just as I'm ready to tell Barb she lost a lot of weight and feign interest in her eating habits, a piercing scream fills the dayroom.

It's Grace. She's trying to leave Sam's cell. Her body is half in, half out. Sam has her by the arm and is jerking her back inside. I stand in alarm.

"For the love of God, Sam, take your pervert hands off her!"

"I'm no pre-vert sombitch." Sam articulates.

"Sit down, Janie, there is nothing you can do," Keisha said. "Grace is a grown woman. I saw her sitting on Sam's lap earlier. She probably agreed to trade a chick-let for some deplorable sexual favor and now it's time to pay the piper. That girl is used to learning things the hard way."

I stood glaring at Sam's closed cell door. I shuddered and heaved a deep sigh. I dropped back down in my seat with an air of forbearance reconciled to the fact that Keisha was right. Shaking off the nausea, I focused on the game.

"What do you have," asked Barb.

I laid down my cards revealing a two, seven, Jack, nine, and a five. The hand was in various suits making it more pretty than practical.

When all hands are revealed my partner sits serenely with a royal flush, ace-high straight flush in the suit of hearts, displayed neatly before her. It was a thing of beauty.

I find myself completely forgetting about the rape in progress. I grinned widely. It stirs one's vanity to fool people and selfishness has a ferocious appetite. Leaning forward, I dragged the pot into our already big fat pile. These winnings consisted of several stamps, an orange soda, cheese doodles, and three Chick-O-Sticks. Oh sweet prosperity.

I felt the poisonous greed pulsing through my veins. It feels fabulous. Greed is my most favorite of the seven deadliest. The moment winnings slip into my covetous fingers an imaginary pillar rises within me. I walk with an air of competency. I look more attractive and grow several inches taller. Everything glows and glitters making all things right with the human race.

TEN

Because I'm a lady, it would be unbecoming of me to describe ItsHella County Jails indoor lockup as a shithole. Relevance aside, I believe it would show poor taste and bad manners. It is better that I describe it as an elaborate manmade ecological unit which is domicile to hundreds of people, millions of mice, and a gazillion cockroaches. A delicate balance exists among the three species, each living with, and accidently swallowing the fecal matter of the other.

I'm approaching month six of my stay in this malaria pond. During this time, I've been permitted to go outdoors twice for air, recreation, and exercise. Too much of the indoor makes us white folk pallid. If we don't receive our recommended daily allowance of vitamin D, we can become see through.

The outdoor recreation area is a narrow enclosure surrounded by brick building. It consists of a concrete slab and can best be described as a breezeway. Due to lack of roominess, activities are limited to standing upright. It's in this little piece of heaven that one can find the tattered remains of broken promises and the first hopeful sprout of grass appearing through cracked concrete as nature attempts to recoup what's rightfully hers.

Unsentenced inmates aren't permitted to work. To help pass the time, I attended every available church service. It didn't matter which denomination. I found a measure of redemption in them all. Church service stirs curious emotions within. It's an environment able to affect the hardest of hardboiled.

I often encourage the girls to come with me. A temporary reprieve from this asylum setting might do them some good. This is often met with righteous anger.

"Catholic services, Ladies." I announce. "Anyone want to come with?"

"What in the hell do they know about our suffering?" Barb cries. Barb is an instigator.

I find myself surrounded by five women. They have the look and feel of an angry mob just itching for a fight.

"Screw that noise," cries Hazel. "I don't trust those child molesting priests with their smooth black coats and neatly starched collars. Their bodies are warm and bellies are always full. They got plenty of other people's money in their pockets. How dare those perverts lecture us?"

"How dare they." Barb says, egging the group on. She loves this.

I give her a look. She gives me a raised eyebrow and a smirk.

"Yeah, what the hell do they know," cries another in outrage.

Oh boy. Already I'm sorry I brought it up.

"The Catholic Church is intent on expunging sexuality as if it were some vile sin or a crime." Barb said. "Look at Mary, the Mother of Jesus Christ, the Virgin Mother. I'm no English Major but I know an oxymoron when I hear one. How do they get away with such nonsense? They, who have shown us time and time again that they are nothing more than a band of legitimized sexual predators."

"You got that right." Yolanda bellows.

She's a Christian and often attends services with me. She must've forgotten.

"Those freaky freaks," she continues. "How can they relate to our struggles? Has that priest ever been evicted, tossed to the curb with three kids and had no place to go?"

"Hell no!" Barb pipes up eager to sow discord in her wake.

"The catholic church is one of the greatest contributors to women's oppression. They don't support women. They are self interested and organized. They are steeped in predatory greed and neck deep in privilege. The church and everything it stands for sickens me!"

Ouch. Yes, of course it's unfair. Women populate the pews in a catholic church in great numbers. Despite this, the church remains steadfast in their tradition of treating women as second-class citizens. Women are banned from positions of power because they are considered inferior in both status and rights when compared to men.

Women see this. They know but they don't care. They understand that these silly dictates are a product of the ego and that ego functions out of fear. They understand that the authorities know not what they do. And so, it's best they not be taken too seriously.

You can be sure women understand plenty. They spend a lifetime ovulating, cramping, giving birth, and bleeding that is later followed by a rude dose of menopause. These mortifications humble women and help to ground them to certain reality, namely, that there is an infinite intelligence that is in us and all around us, which is beyond any mere mortals ability to comprehend.

This chaotic material world, a thing not of spirit, is a mishmash of booby traps, every cunning craftiness, and sleight of hand. The wicked lie in wait to deceive. This is why women pray, and tithe, and worship. Prayer is a safety net that women hope will cover them and more importantly, those they love. Every Good Mother is a warrior. She needs no stupid shiny medal to prove it. My Mother is such a woman. For this I count myself blessed.

The door slides open and I step out into the hallway. Yolanda, Georgia, and a thuggish girl with tats follow me. An officer shackles us and leads us down the corridor to the chapel. We sit in metal folding chairs and wait for the priest to enter. Yolanda reaches over and takes my hand.

"I didn't mean all that mess I said back at the Pod. Barb has a way of working people up."

"Yeah, I know."

"I'm gonna tell God I'm sorry." Yolanda let go of my hand, made the sign of the cross, and closed her eyes.

When the priest entered, Yolanda elbows me.

"Here comes the pervert." She whispers.

We giggle.

+++

The majority of unsentenced prisoners rarely stay indoors for longer than a couple weeks. I've been here for almost six months. I think that I'm in big trouble.

Indoor lockup is typically a layover for those en route to tent city, State/Federal Prison, or the Arizona State Hospital. The last destination explains why there are so many crackpots. These are the Rule 11's, the girls who never approached the door tagged "Normal". Mostly they are injured souls damaged hideously in their early years. Their childhoods were a cavalcade of abuse. They were brought into this world by the warm embrace of monsters that showered them with endless servings of disappointment. These girls have seen terror and those who see terror may commit terrors equally as terrifying.

A Rule 11 is one who's deemed incompetent to stand trial due to a determination that they are unable to understand the proceedings against them. Their court appointed defense attorneys have filed a motion requesting that the inmate undergo a Rule 11 evaluation, as outlined under the Arizona Rule 11, Mental Competency Laws. Consequently, long-term indoor lockup placement is similar in many ways to being committed to a mental asylum.

+++

Georgia keeps the habits of sanity and the intonation of reason. She's an Asian woman who's as American as Connie Chung. She recently turned sixty. Her face is smooth and free of wrinkles. Age was marked with shadows that adversity and suffering lend to the face. On the surface, Georgia is polite and capable, but if at any point crossed, she became as unstable as wet feet on a marble floor. Georgia is here under Rule 11. She has been here for eight months.

Georgia moves about with an aura of resignation and has acclimated herself well to this environment. It's obvious that she doesn't really belong here. You can tell she has all the street smarts of a punctured tire. Despite this, she shared a contentment that I've noticed in others who find jail a more satisfying circumstance than the one from which they came. One so long confined often finds comfort in their restraint. Freedom and release become difficult and undesirable.

The longer one is here the more normal it becomes. The less strange the residents seem to be. It's the case where familiarity breeds indifference. This is a sober world without any filters. It may be crass and in your face, but there is something very truthful and straightforward about it.

That the outside world is looking down on us is of no consequence. In an effort to protect a civilized society, we're placed behind bars. Inadvertently, we too are protected from situations and the society. For many, prison is less complex, more predictable, well ordered, and safe.

Incarceration offers a valuable life-changing lesson for those with eyes to see. Confinement puts one in a position where we can no longer avoid or ignore a basic truth. We aren't on this planet to be satisfied or to seek fulfillment through conditions. Peace comes when we rise above the conditions and simply accept. By transcending the conditions internally, we suddenly discover that conditions are relatively agreeable. To no longer, be in respect of want, we are happy with whatever state we are, therefore to be content.

Georgia is being held on charges of aggravated assault with a deadly weapon. She flew into a rage and attacked her husband of thirty years.

"He is always drunk and I'm far too sober." Georgia explained. "You try listening to the same damn story for three decades and see if you don't start yielding a knife."

It seemed like a persuasive constitutional argument to me.

Walter is Georgia's husband. Georgia referred to herself as Walters' surrogate-spine. I wasn't sure if this was funny or tragic.

Walter puts money on Georgia's books and visits her religiously. He wasn't the one who called the police. When Walter arrived at the hospital via ambulance he was rushed into the emergency room. When it was discovered that Walter had the handle of a butter knife protruding from his abdomen the authorities were contacted.

Walter misses Georgia's abuse and wants her to come back home where she belongs. Georgia, on the other hand, has settled in nicely and content to be right where she is.

Every morning, without fail, Georgia uses my sink to fill her cup with hot water.

"Is your sink broken, Georgia?"

"I only get cold water."

"I can look at that." The butch in me said.

"Oh my, that would be very nice of you."

I beam.

When Georgia was done filling her cup, I hop off the top bunk and head to her cell.

I need to be needed. Finally, here is something. I follow behind her with a lighthearted sense of purpose, my ego lifting me.

When we reached her cell, I walked to the sink. With my right hand, I pushed the button to the right, just above the sink. With my left hand, I felt the cold water flowing from the spigot. Then, with my left hand, I pushed the button to the left, just above the sink. Using my right hand, I felt the water warm then gradually heat up.

"NO, NO, NO!" Georgia reprimands, "I'm right handed!"

She is suggesting that I had the audacity to imply otherwise. Georgia's behavior was a bit of a wild card.

"Ohhhh, okay." I say brightly.

My work here was done. I turn and go.

The following morning, like clockwork, Georgia enters my cell. We exchange routine pleasantries and she heads to the sink. With the right thumb of her right hand, she presses the button on the right side just above the sink. When her cup runneth over she says, "thank you."

"Don't mention it."

The occasional little quirk aside, Georgia typically hovered within the bounds of reason, except when she attacked a bible. She said it was staring at her. In her defense, I saw the bible in question. It stared at me too.

ELEVEN

What people think of me is certainly none of my business. In a perfect world, I'd be invisible. If I must be visible then I simply wish to be ignored. I like to live like a mouse in my jail cell, making no noise, leaving no trace (or not much). A quiet life is what I like. Mild pleasures and uncomplicated solitude are all my simple soul demands. I have a need, whenever possible, to keep away from the crowd.

It's hard to be alone here. It isn't as if you have the excuse of a busy day to discourage interlopers. Why people insist on being a bother, I shall never understand. It's the darndest thing in life, the people that you most particularly want to slither away from insist on clustering around you like mosquito's to a picnic. You know how it is, bores insist on telling you what baloney does to their digestive organs and codgers try to touch you.

I, like many, am a big fan of the Book of Proverbs for messages such as this: "withdraw thy foot from the house of thy neighbor, lest having his fill he hate thee".

Amen to that.

As I write this, I can see in my periphery that a source of irritation is headed my way. Really, one gets about as much privacy in this place as a public toilet seat. Now I have to put on a friendly manner and behave as if I were a nicer person than I actually am.

The annoyance in route has just left a table of five busybody yentas. For the past ten minutes, these women have been sporadically shooting a collective exploratory eye in my direction. I noticed their minds were reeling with misconceptions and abysmal value judgments.

Yentas are not a reliable source. In this circle, feelings take priority over facts and generalities outrank concrete evidence.

Idle women are always ready to mind other people's business. This gossipy environment had the feel of what it must be like to be trapped inside a Jane Austen novel.

As the pain in my butt approaches, the yentas sit eagerly attentive looking on with great anticipation. I sat contently alone with a pencil in my mouth surrounded by papers. I mentally prepared myself for aggravation.

This nuisance was already making my mood bitter.

When dipshit reached my table, she looks down at me with a judgmental glower. Her hands are planted firmly on her ample hips. Her bearing was that of a woman who has been sent in to dismantle a thermonuclear bomb.

I removed the pencil from my lips and tilt my head upward to meet her smug knowing. The corners of my mouth curl up in a forced grin. One should be polite, I suppose. I don't think there was anything in my manner that would suggest that I would've liked to stick her in the neck with my pencil. Nevertheless, behind my calm front simmered the apprehension that always seized me when approached by someone I don't wish to keep amused.

"Why are you always writing?"

She's leaning in with an accusing glare.

Here it comes. I remained silent and readied myself for the absurd.

"You're an undercover cop aren't you? Admit it! Everybody knows it!"

There was a hush of delighted horror around the yenta's table. I forced my gaze downward to the Kool-Aid stained Formica tabletop. I briefly close my eyes, suck in some air, and will myself not to laugh. Keeping my face expressionless required great effort.

This place is a trip. It's a culture of fear and distrust. Everyone is looking over their shoulder at everyone else. It doesn't matter if you're doing time or collecting a paycheck. Everyone is suspect. My being a plant was rumored many months ago and has developed into an absolute truth. What's most preposterous is that these blundering jailbirds think they warrant such examination. I'm reminded of a quote from the great and very funny Mark Twain: "What gets us into trouble is not what we don't know; it is what we know for sure that just ain't so."

"We want to know what you're writing about!" she demands.

"I'm not a cop." I state for the umpteenth time.

"For God's sake," cried the bother. "Tell the truth."

"God," I quote here, "is not the author of confusion but of peace."

The know-nothing's face radiated puzzlement.

"Don't change the subject, just admit it, you're a LIAR!" She hollers banging a fist on the table. This show of bravado causes the Yenta's to squeal in delight.

"You tell her," cries a co-conspirator.

Well okay then, if I'm going to be called a liar, I may as well make an effort to deserve the title. In the words of the late great Harry Truman: "If you can't convince them, confuse them."

I drew in a deep breath and look up at the irritation with a face I typically reserve for puppies.

She found my infective smile disarming, the defiance drained out of her. Lifting myself from my seat, I leaned over the table and closer to her.

"If you promise not to tell your friends, I'll tell you everything."

"Oh, OH of course," she said with conspiratorial coolness. "You can totally trust me."

I sat down and motioned with my eyes suggesting she do the same. She settled down in the seat directly across the table from me. She leaned forward with all the warmth of a crackling fire on a frosty night. If I had been her filthy rich Aunt, she couldn't have been more palsy-walsy. She was my new BFF.

"Why, the moment I saw you I thought to myself, now, there is a woman that anyone can trust. I must say I can't remember when I've last seen such an honest face."

"Well, I'm not surprised at all."

She was tremendously taken with herself. I seemed to have hit on her favorite subject.

"You know, complete strangers come right up to ME and tell ME their entire life story."

"You must be an enormous comfort to one and all."

I showered her with a look of admiration.

"Oh, I certainly seem to be. People just love to tell ME every little sordid detail as if they've known ME all their life. Maybe I'm too trusting."

"That's complete nonsense."

"Oh, well, you know sometimes I do wonder. Anyway, there must be something about ME that makes people want to bear their souls, just spill their..."

Oh boy, if she was permitted to continue she might go on practically until further notice. Too much more of this self-interested ME fest and I was sure to experience stomach complications.

It was necessary to call her to order with a "Yes, yes, yes, I get the idea. You certainly do have that indefinable something, something, which makes for the Good Samaritan." I lied.

I held up a restrictive hand when she opened her mouth to prattle on. She closed the mouth and looked dumbfounded.

"So, Ellen. It is Ellen?"

"Why, yes it is."

I reached for my pencil and a fresh sheet of paper. On the top left side, I wrote a capital "E".

Looking at her thoughtfully, I apologize and ask, "Do you spell that with one "L" or two?"

Instantly the eyes widened.

"Oh my, no worries this just helps me to remember."

"Oh, of course," she said, relief reshaping her face. "I'm terrible at names too. So, anyway, have you dug up any really good dirt on anyone in here?"

"Oh my God" "Oh my God," I repeated with wide eyes and exaggerated annunciation. Lowering my voice and leaning forward I say, "You aren't going to believe what goes on around this place."

I look left, then right, then back to Ellen. I lean in even closer and drop my tone lower still.

"The scandal and moral depravity boggles the mind. If I hadn't discovered these things first hand, I would've never believed it myself. It's collusion most fowl and it's going on right under our very noses!"

I paused for the cause and racked my brain for additional superlatives. Then I thought better of it. One must be careful not to overdo.

Ellen's green eyes went wide with possibility. Hers was the look of a woman who had just been handed an enormous cardboard check from Ed McMahon.

"Would you just look at me going on and on about things I've no business even talking about. Where are my manners?" I exclaim.

"Oh, not at all, please go on."

"And there you are just being as nice as pie, allowing me to monopolize the entire conversation. I should be ashamed of myself. Me, me, me, enough already about me! Let's talk about you. What do you think about me? Ha, ha, I'm just playing. For reals, tell me are you a Native to Arizona?"

With bated breath and a look of expectancy, I went mute.

"But...but...well, gosh, I'm not very interesting?" Ellen confessed.

"I'm sure that isn't true at all, Ellen. You know, actually I was kind of wondering, now that we're friends and all, I was kind of wondering if...but I just couldn't."

"If, If what?" Ellen asked with a compelling eagerness.

"I just wanted to ask you a personal question. But it's stupid. I'm sorry, never mind."

"There are no stupid questions." Ellen said as if that were true. "Please go right ahead. You can ask me anything, anything at all."

"Well okay." And in my best Perry Mason voice, I interrogated: "On the day that you were apprehended, is there anything you failed to admit to the arresting officer? We're on to you fresh meat. I advise you to use your loaf and start singing like a canary or the next seat you get will offer a wet sponge cap and a gazillion watts of electricity!"

Before I had the chance to say, 'ha, ha, just kidding,' Ellen was out of her seat and half way to her cell. She seemed to be in an awful hurry. The way she scuttled off you would've thought that I had just offered her a nice, hot, steamy mug of tuberculosis.

"Hey Ellen," I hollered at her disappearing rear end. "Where are you going? I like you! I was going to turn you in last."

PART II
TENT CITY

TWELVE

"Free at last, free at last, Thank God Almighty." I'm free at last. Month six, the Judge finally sentenced me to one year in tent city. The previous six months don't count toward my sentence and in fact, it's as if they never actually occurred. And to this I say, oh, okay.

The offending charges for which I've been found guilty are as follows: two separate felony counts, burglary, and one separate felony count, trafficking of stolen goods.

I hope this does not sully your excellent opinion of me. Then again, I suppose it is best that I face facts straight away. With three felony convictions, it's going to be hard to bounce a quarter off my reputation.

The good news is I'm getting the hell out of here. Compared to indoor lockup, tent city is an all expense paid trip to Disneyland with a Mickey escort. The bright Arizona sun is a disinfectant that I've sorely need. Not only do I get to go alfresco, that's where I'll be living.

I don't wish to leave you with the impression that I was pleased about the one-year sentence. I wasn't. One year worth of pressing the forehead against a fence and I'll have chain-link indentations on the brow for the rest of my life. The news put me in the foulest of dispositions. The way I see it I have a lot of brooding to do. I found myself in one of those moods where life suddenly becomes irksome. The future stretched out empty and depressing before me. I would've liked to drop off the face of the earth.

It's in such a frame of mind that I typically turn to drugs. In here, drugs are but a nuisance. No, instead I'll resort to what has always sustained me in the past, distraction.

I've always been a workaholic. Soon, I'll be assigned a job. I'm looking forward to exercising my compulsive disorder. Work is what I wanted. Ha! Just let them try to make my life more difficult then I intend to make it for myself! Work is precisely what the doctor ordered. You won't catch me eating the bread of idleness. No siree Bob. I'll work like a woman possessed. I'll gladly sow like a fool that others may reap. I'll transform any "to do" list into "too done". I'll toil like a maniac all day on whatever mindless, menial, retarded task I'm assigned. I'll thrive in the deadening effects of mundane repetition.

And if necessity arises, I'll pick up the slack of the good-for-nothing loafers. I'll do their work, my work, and then I'll work some more. Everyone knows that drudgery is the price of virtue.

After I work my fingers to the bone, I'll dine on nutrient-free food. Then I'll steal away to my bunk and write. I'll write until my fingers bleed and my eyes refused to cooperate. Surely, I'll look back on this time and come to feel it was all for the best. Everyone knows a person must go through the fire before they can write their masterpiece. Who is it that said, "We learn in suffering what we teach in song?" I can't remember.

Lessons of life amount not to good judgment. Hell no. The best lessons are a product of outrageous mistakes, embarrassing transgressions, and unsightly scar tissue. It's in feeling the iron hand of circumstance close tightly around my throat that I get that old second wind. The return of relative ease of breathing after one realizes they are still alive and things can't possibly get any worse. Janie Jane Doe Doughy, the woman, might be a miserable, hopeless ruin of a human being with a crumpled soul heavy laden with regret and remorse. But, Janie Doughy, the fascinating protagonist and soon to be phenomenal Author, will turn out such a novel of murkiness that it will leave the most sophisticated critic blubbering ceaselessly.

I can see it now. My adoring public will clamor for copies until overly enthusiastic admirers turn my doorway into a useless pile of woodchips. Hence, only then will I feel that all this torment was really a blessing in disguise. But, then again, I doubt it.

I'm afraid I might've gotten a little carried away here.

+++

Inmates are placed in tents according to job assignments. Those awaiting a job opening are placed in the welfare tent. Typically, the stay isn't more than a couple days. Jailhouse duties include, but aren't limited to, laundry, kitchen, dog kennels, and dayroom trustees. Each tent houses approximately twenty-five women with the exception of the laundry tent (a.k.a. The mansion) which holds forty-four.

Inside the tents are metal, two-tier bunk beds flanking left and right, leaving a narrow passage in the center as a thoroughfare. There is a large industrial fan mounted high at one end of each tent. In the summer months, this appliance is largely decorative. Death by climate change was my chief concern.

Woods person or not, all sentenced inmates earn a position in a large, moldy, OD green, army tent whose roofs are speckled with holes. These gaps in the canvas serve as a constant reminder that rain would suck. Naturally, from previous rains the mildew activated by the moisture has left an unpleasant aroma. Here you can experience what it must feel like to sleep in a giant unwashed jockstrap.

I don't mind it so much. It takes me right back to Army Boot camp. It makes me nostalgic. This experience does not charm everyone.

A severe medical condition may rescue the disenchanted inmate from the ill-fated campsite setting. Leprosy, hemorrhoids, or non-dormant genital herpes are just a few ailments an inmate might hope for, landing them in a cozy cell inside the jail. A nice temperature controlled environment undisturbed by weather and all its consequences.

The medieval care, I mean medical care here at ItsHella is topnotch. It isn't antiquated, hardly at all. In fact, you can rest assured that if, GOD FORBID, anything were to happen to you the medical staff will use only the highest quality black market explosives to jangle those freeloading evil spirits right out of your cranium. Ha, ha, I tease. Exorcisms and ritual killings are only available through the jail's ministry services.

Upon my arrival to tent city, I was placed in the welfare tent. It turned out to be a pleasant experience. Two days of rest and reading while rising at the crack of noon. Sadly, welfare tent living isn't all skittles and beer. In the real world, welfare recipients are looked down upon, thought to be shiftless and lazy. The same applies here. The disapproving criticism and unbridled looks of loathing are coming from crackhead losers, making it slightly harder to take.

On the third day, I was assigned to the laundry. I tried it. I didn't like it. It lasted two days.

Now, don't get me wrong. I like to work toll-free as much as the next person. Lord knows the past its sell-by-date food provided is payment enough.

Laundry is a backbreaking, laborious undertaking. Let's face facts. I'm no spring chicken. In dog years, I'd be dead already. It's best that I not be overworked, either mentally or physically. Great and important changes are occurring in my rapidly deteriorating cadaver and nature should not be overtaxed.

Laundering is hard, hot, and dangerous involving hot dryers and scratchy, unhygienic fabric. What's worse and unthinkable is the necessity of handling underwear containing aged fecal matter and congealed menstrual blood of the unwashed masses. Obviously, a Petri dish of deadly diseases much like the bubonic plague can rankle. This task requires special training and a Hazmat suit. OSHA Hazardous Materials Waste Management Certification Training is all I'm asking for here. Otherwise, sorry no can do.

Some prefer laundry work over any other kind. The laundry workers are allowed a better diet and permitted to have second and third helpings. I don't believe in seconds. Thirds are an abomination.

I never really liked laundry. I'm not ashamed to admit that on the outs, I buried most of my dirty clothes in the backyard with those pots and pans that looked too hard to clean.

Greenhorns coming into the laundry are placed on the folding tables. I for one don't know how to fold. If it isn't a towel, I need a hanger.

A large circular analog clock is mounted in clear view of the folding station. Its big hand rotates two minutes forward then eight minutes back all throughout the day. A timepiece that has been worn thin by desperate stares. It refuses to die. To look at it was to feel the countless decades of inmate eyes reflected in it. Time, illusory yet indestructible, inches forward mocking those who will it to hurry the hell up.

Folding isn't the only mind-numbing task in this sweltering armpit of a work environment. If you hope to progress to a more agreeable chore you must kiss the posterior of a senior inmate. In return, this nimrod, which you're now indebted, will put a good word in for you with the guard.

Homey don't kiss ass. Getting chummy for a better shit-job was not in the stars for me.

I'm no quitter. When life hands me a yeast infection, I make biscuits. However, this laundry work, as my Mother would put it, "is shit for the birds". Whatever that means and that's exactly how I felt.

So, on the morning of day three of laundry detail I decided to be a no-show. Upon hearing the announcement over the crackling public address system, "ALL LAUNDRY WORKERS REPORT TO THE DAYROOM", I, in traditional Zen fashion, did nothing.

Forty or so laundry workers are cuffed and marched toward the laundry facility. After which time, a guard will check the laundry tent for sick call, no good, good for nothings. This is where I come in.

As I sit on my bunk waiting for the inevitable, my mind raced and stomach turned. Despite the sweltering desert heat, my feet got colder by the second.

I was staring absently at my feet when I noticed the shoes. That's one good thing came out of the stupid laundry detail. Once you have a job, you're permitted to trade in your flip-flops for a pair of blue canvas sneakers. This makes my after dinner stroll around the yard more enjoyable. At every couple of steps, gravel tends to lodge between the flip-flop and the sole of the foot, making these beachcombers an impediment to an aerobic workout. Getting a pair of canvas shoes had been a real treat. I smile down at the footwear as if they were responsible for being there.

Looking up, I notice that I'm the only one in the tent. Instantly, I find myself right back to my disagreeable reality. I started second guessing myself. I feel sure I've made a grave mistake. Closing my eyes, I slowly recite an Our Father.

Just yesterday, a female inmate who refused to work was shoved up against the wall, cuffed with force enough to cause bloodshed, and manhandled by a female officer who screamed, "IF I TELL YOU TO WORK. YOU GO TO WORK!" If I get roughed-up, at least it won't be in front of a live audience. Oddly, this thought doesn't make me feel better.

I'm in the habit of imagining terrible things that never come to pass. It's high time that I take control of my thoughts and emotions. I'm reminded of one of my favorite quotes from Mark Twain: "I have been through some terrible things in my life, some of which actually happened."

After all, what if they send a nice guard to mediate? A guard with the mind of a truly illumined might approach me and ask, "My dear child, why have you not joined your sisters?"

And I'd reply in earnest, "I don't really feel like it." I'd, no doubt, be praised for 'keeping it real'. The entire ordeal would end in a warm embrace, followed by a poignant duet as we sing in perfect harmony, "Kum Bay Yah".

Let's be realistic. Guards are the fly in everyone's ointment. They are the mosquito's that muck-up our long awaited picnic. They are scary and mean. They assert their authority in an annoyingly domineering way concerning all matters, petty and trivial. Completely void of empty-threats, they parade about with a 'Don't make me say it twice', pompous attitude. You can always tell a prison guard by the total vacancy upon which occupies the space where normal people have a facial expression.

I was sitting on my bunk nervous and seized with dread when I heard the sound of tactical footwear walking deliberately in my direction.

CONDITION: Code Red

Crying doesn't work in this place and being dead is no excuse. I felt a peculiar sense of terror climbing me like a creeping plant. It's never easy to properly prepare oneself for a situation fraught with embarrassing potentiality. I remained sitting on my bunk stiffly and barely breathing. I was trying to appear nondescript and unremarkable to avoid being noticed. Despite my best efforts, the officer saw me

105

immediately. My presence in that empty tent was as obvious as poop in a sugar bowl.

With a disapproving attitude, the officer marches in my direction. As I stood to greet her, I could feel the blood drain from my face.

The officer's hand-on-tazor stance and tight-lipped severity was my clue that it wasn't a good time to ask for a hug. Filled with the courage that comes with desperation, I beamed civilly and opened the conversation welcomingly.

"Good morning, Officer. You look marvelous. Have you lost weight?"

"Well, I..." she started, seeming pleased with herself then just as quickly, she came to her senses.

I braced myself for an unpleasant scene.

She eyed me narrowly and in a tone as heavy as a bag of cement she said, "You're expected to be en route to laundry detail. Why are you still here?"

Two bits say this woman has never been the life and soul of any social gathering. Hers was an inner hardness that, if I had one ounce of common sense, would know better than to trifle with. This is where I often fall short.

"Ah, Officer," I bantered brightly, "you and your infinite expectations. If you don't mind me saying, you do seem dreadfully uptight. Officiousness is the curse of any government job. It isn't really who you are."

I pause here to put on a sympathetic frown.

"May I recommend tranquility to you? A life that's burdened with expectations and inflexibility is a ponderous life indeed. Its fruits are misery and discontent. In tranquility, you can be one with Mother Earth, your creator, and yourself. Its rewards are inner peace, joy, and love that flows like a river. And, Officer," I say with soft eyes. "You'd be amazed how a little bit of love goes a long, long way."

It seemed that my spongy words of encouragement caused the officer's face to turn a purplish crimson. I noticed a vein in her neck begin to pulsate uncontrollably. This was a woman wound tighter than a garage door spring. She fell into a silence that seemed a mixture of chilly and disturbing.

"Officer," are you okay?"

And that's when she flattened me, smashing my face into the cement slab floor of the tent. The pain drew the breath right out of my lungs. The whole episode was jarring and extremely unpleasant.

Officer Bossypants cuffed me. I was jerked to my feet and hastily pulled to the dayroom. There I sat staring dumbly into space for hours on end pondering what possible lesson I might glean from this fresh new indignity. I factored the moral of this horror story down to its lowest common denominator.

Talk shit, get hit.

Another officer finally showed up to walk me to my next extremely undesirable life situation, solitary confinement.

THIRTEEN

Oh the horror of being alone. In the hole, one is free to marinate in boredom while vacantly waiting for the next thing not to happen. Here we learn just how weary one becomes of their own company.

You'll also have countless hours to ponder some of life's deeply vital questions.

Why do I exist? When do I get to die? If it's better to broil, then why do I fry? Is there a God? Why am I queer? If I'm walking backwards, is my butt still my rear?

These are just of few of my biggies.

In lonesome captivity, it's just you and that voice inside your head. It has you cornered. This abysmal poltergeist remains stuck in a tape loop criticizing, judging, and incriminating you for your every action and omission. A cataloging of shame and blame that pulls on you continuously like gravity.

With great momentum, the intellect generates a flurry of negative thoughts that jerk you to and fro like a human chew toy in the mouth of a Nazi German Shepherd. Furious, you demand that the voice in your head cease and desist, pronto. Returning anger with anger, the voice tells you to go to hell. Startled by reproof you apologize.

"Lockdown Status" means you're in a disturbingly cramped 2-person cell for 23 hours of the day, for a predetermined period, normally 30 days, sometimes less. Whether you have a cellmate or not depends entirely on influx. You may have none or as many as four making a trip to the potty reason for alarm. Those with the least seniority get a piece of floor space that they must share with rodents, bugs, and whatever filth might come splashing out of the commode.

Nothing belongs to us as completely as time. And you'll have oodles of it to review the flimsiness of your earthly existence. Freedom in which to examine the enormous gap between who you are and who your devastated parents had wished you'd become. Here you can observe yourself getting older and older, gradually sliding into decay, while

108

growing deeper and deeper into despair. Look, no hands -- your entire miserable, purposeless life swiftly spiraling down a flushing toilet. The Book of Ezekiel says it flawlessly: "There you will remember your conduct and all the actions by which you have defiled yourselves, and you will loathe yourselves for all the evil you have done."

Suicide, like yawning, is contagious. In the hole the mind slips into the subject of self-deliverance as naturally as a hand slips into a pocket. Death is freedom, the final remedy. No forwarding address aside, death is a real win-win.

"He who dies pays all his debts." That is somewhere in the Bible...or was that Shakespeare? Either way, I find the statement very encouraging.

Many residing in state institutions regard death as a great endowment because it kicks open all the doors and windows.

Penal institutions are required to guarantee a suicide-proof setting. Without said precautions, there would be an epidemic of self-killings in here. No big deal you might say. Indeed. However, you fail to regard one important factor. The State of Arizona doesn't pay the county good money to house and feed corpses.

My next cell-door neighbor repeatedly smashed her head against steel bars and gave herself a coma. We all heard her throw herself against the bars several times. We heard her grunt and groan, then slide to the floor. And then, we heard nothing at all.

Nobody in the ward uttered a syllable. We were understandably stunned but more tastelessly curious. I'm not sure how much time passed between her final sighs of anguish and her being discovered by a guard making scheduled rounds. We all watched from our cells as the medical staff took her out in a stretcher. She was bloody and blue lipped but breathing. I must say she couldn't have looked deader.

When this brave soldier finds out that she won't be appearing in tomorrow's obituary column, she'll be disappointed.

It isn't like I didn't understand. I've broken down more than once myself anchored to the idea of sinking. I know just how low one can go. Everyone here knows. They know too that the next attempt might be theirs.

This was a woman of cast iron ovaries. Very impressive indeed! Dead or alive, she has earned our respect. Whether our potentially brain damaged sister knows it or not that stunt got her a warm, comfy cozy bed in the infirmary. When or if she comes to she might also win an all expense paid trip to the nut wing. I hear it's real nice. Good for her! You have to admire that kind of "can die" determination.

I'm not proud to admit that her achievement left me feeling inadequate. Nobody likes a show off. Here I sit a hardened criminal to a-scared to bang my head. I'd rather pill myself to eternal sleep. Where pain is concerned, you can count me out. I've never really liked it. I'm pathetic. People like me give places like this a bad name.

For those with thin skin, the reptilian "always cold", this place is a fricken nightmare. Willing your blood to circulate faster doesn't help. Glaring at the belching air vent won't correct the problem either. Feel free to ask for an extra blanket. While you're at it, you might as well ask for a fist full of barbiturates, a fifth of Jack, and reservations at Sedona's Luxury Day Spa. All unanswered requests will leave you wide-awake and inches from death by hypothermia.

While you're awake, you can listen to the relaxing sounds of a lunatic two cells down shrieking because she has nightmares, is suffering the sweats and mental spiders of withdrawal, or is terrified because her daddy has come into her cell through the air vent and is now raping her. A scream similar to that of a mother watching her baby being fed into a wood chipper. The shrieking cries are typically accompanied by, now woke inmates, shouting curse words and death threats. It isn't unusual for this never-ending loop of agitated chatter to go on all day and night.

In the interest of appearing civilized, a grievance officer is available upon request. Grievance procedures are a means of dispute resolution. Inmates who believe they have been wrongly accused and unjustly segregated use it to address complaints. I took the liberty to exercise my rights jurisprudence and requested a grievance form.

In the limited space provided I put down the conversation I had with that ill-tempered guard, word for word. Additionally, I proposed all guards be closely scrutinized and under stringent government control. Something must be done to prevent fellow inmates from being subjected to the disgraceful insult and outrage that I endured. I also pointed out the high risk of this discourteous behavior negatively affecting morale. With warranted vindication, I submitted my grievance form.

The next time I saw this form, it was in the hands of an actual human being. I felt certain that document would be routed to a shredder. Once again, I'm mistaken.

Officer Justice Forall was a black man, very tall and frightfully serious. He stood at my door with grievance in hand. I issued a cheery smile coupled with a bright verbal salutation. Neither was reciprocated. This came as no real surprise. You can already see where this was headed. I braced myself for the unpleasant.

Officer Forall opens my cell door and asked me to take a seat in the dayroom. He sat directly across from me. The stoic administrator looked over my grievance form with the seriousness of a mortician. When he was done, he removed his wired framed glasses and laid them on the table.

Looking at me with competent, reasonable eyes he said, "Your grievance submission says much, but tells me little. I've come to understand that you're here because you refused to go to work. Is this true?"

"Well, Officer, I didn't refuse in actual words. However, my actions may have hinted at that possibility."

"That sounds like a yes."

"Well, yes. I mean no. I mean yes and no." I said shrugging my shoulders and smiling feebly.

"You'll need to pick one."

"It isn't that simple, Officer. I do want to work. Work is an agreeable distraction which will help to make time pass more quickly. This is a thing I most certainly welcome. It is working in the laundry for which I'm opposed."

"I see," nodded the delightful gentleman. "Did you explain this to the detention officer that wrote you up?"

"Uhmmm, well no, no I didn't."

"And why not?"

"Because she was scary stern and I felt that I may have been in the wrong in the first place. The thing rather put me on edge. When I get nervous I tend to babble incessantly. This nervous talk works as a calming mechanism."

I diverted my eyes to the table. Shame rushed over me like a blush.

"Nervous talkers are you?"

"That's exactly right. I find myself going on and on about the most absurd things." I confessed to the tabletop. "I can't seem to help myself and what's more, I don't understand why I do it. I only know that it is rarely well received, especially around the overly severe. Between you and me," I said looking at the officer. "I think the guard was merely trying to shut me up." Leaning in conspiratorially I added, "I can't say that I blame her."

With that, Officer Forall checked a small square at the bottom of the grievance form. Sliding the form toward me, he pointed with the pen and said, "Sign here."

"Sure." I said. Taking the pen, I scribbled my autograph.

He stood.

I stood.

He walked toward my cell.

I followed.

He opens the door to my dreary chamber. I stepped in. Somehow, I felt oddly lighter, almost buoyant. It is as if I was granted a slight reprieve from what strains life had been putting upon me. That was a lovely visit. He was an awfully nice man.

The officer locked my cage and turned to go.

"Excuse me, Officer, when will I be getting out of here?" I say to his back.

He turns. "How long have you been in the hole so far?"

"Two days."

"Just subtract that number from thirty."

"But, that's an eternity."

"It will only seem like it."

And with that, my new friend was gone.

+++

At some point, I had exhausted all of my precious resources pissing and moaning while taking self-pity to astonishing new heights. My tear ducts were completely void of the fluids necessary to constitute a meaningful cry. Only then did I realize that the hole isn't so bad after all. Here I can learn the true value of sleeping in. How relaxing it is to lie about and be looked after without having to lift a finger. My meals are brought right to my door. If I were at the Ritz, they'd call this room service.

How wonderful to have the luxury of undisturbed thought. Living in the real world with a job, housework, and all those bills there was virtually no time for actual thinking. The thing I have always needed more of in my life turns out to be nothing. Nothing is something worth having. And that's precisely what the hole offers, nothing and plenty of it.

Prison life doesn't have to corrupt. It has not warped my character any more than it already was. In fact, it has allowed me to rise on stepping-stones of my dead self to higher, better things. Worldly battle scars that may break some had armored me for a new lease on life. Everything is about to change. There is going to be brighter days. Whatever this place has to dish out, I can take it.

"Bring it on!" I bellow at the toilet paper clumps that cling to the ceiling. "Bring it on!"

I see now that despair offers a kind of hope. It shines a glaring spotlight on the distance between our appointed happiness and us. Only six months prior, I couldn't have gone two hours without packing my nose full of chemicals. Just look at me now! I'm so better that I completely forgot that I had that problem. It might appear that I've received treatment, which I would've paid heavily for at the Betty Ford Clinic.

I sat with my hands clasped trembling with gratitude. I've never been so stirred in my life. A mighty upheaval has taken place in my soul. A new woman has been born. I had been torn out of the jaws of ruin and delivered from the despair of addiction. My whole world has been changed for me. I don't have to carry the weight of who I've been. I can be free. Counting my blessings one by one, I found the end sum satisfactory.

My parents brought me up religiously. I had the members of the clergy of God to preach to me. I have a place that called me back whenever I strayed to forgive me my sins. No matter how appalling or how many. I feel that pull once more.

It is time to repent. To speak out in words what I've done and thought, sin after sin, the shameful admittance of my stupidity.

The sacrament of penance is meant to relieve the emotional strain of troubled souls. God bless me father for I have sinned, it has been ten years since my last confession. Oh my, this is going to be embarrassing. I can't admit this to a man of the cloth. I don't suppose it would be prudent to lie about how long it's been since my last confession. This would be committing the sin of omission or worse, pride. Nope, it is time to start doing things right. Saint James says, "Whoever keeps the whole law and yet stumbles at just one point are guilty of breaking all of it."

I have learned from a lifetime of being a liar that like a Lay's potato chip, once we indulge, one is never enough. Everyone knows that drug addicts are liars. It is understood that a thief is a liar. Liar, liar pants on fire. There came a point where my entire life was just one big fat bullshit sandwich. My lies were an act of betrayal to those who love me. When I think back on my profound ignorance, I cringe.

I vow to make this my fresh new start. I'll confess all, every sin of deed and thought truthfully. I'll try to sin no more. I'll endeavor to become more like the people I admire.

The thought of this filled me to bursting point with joy. I can do this. Elated, I felt a need to break out in song and at the top of my lungs, I sang.

"This little light of mine I'm gonna let it shine. This little light of mine I'm gonna let it shine. Let it shine, let it shine, let it shine..."

"YOOO, SHUT IT DOWN OR I'LL SHUT IT FOR YOU." shrieked a Godless barbarian a couple cells down.

"That racket's making my ears bleed," shouted an empty-headed birdbrain.

There was additional grumbling throughout that I found distasteful. Like a spelling bee, everyone wanted to get the last word. Well, I refuse to bring myself down to their lev...

"Kiss my ass!" I blurted out involuntarily. Obviously, that couldn't be avoided. It doesn't help my mood knowing that I have no control over myself. My outburst seemed to incite yet another malcontent.

"I know that's you Doughy. Keep it up and I'm going to kick your ass into Thursday."

What? My quick intelligent mind instantly spotted the flaw in that statement. That's two days from now. That isn't even possible. Is it?

I drew myself up haughtily. One shouldn't lose ones temper but the remarks stung me. I bore down coldly at the ceiling that was an outstretched arm away from where I lay. Righteous indignation jerked my shoulders back. You know what this sort of thing does to the spirited woman. Dear friend, I'm the first to admit my shortcomings. That's to say, if I had any. I don't object to fair criticism but this bordered on exploitation. This abuse, if not called to order, could spread like pinkeye.

I mentally inspected a surplus of words in my lexicon of insults. I was prepared to let loose an arsenal of grade school slurs. Choice reprisals flooded the noggin and flowed pass the tongue.

"Oh yeah, you and whose Army? Faah!" and "I know you are but what am I?"

You can be sure I had plenty more where those came from. I was feeling pretty darn brave while in the safety of my locked cell. Those barbarians can't get to me in here.

"Kill me if you can!" I hollered defiantly.

"Keep it up, Dip Shit," a thug threatened.

"Say one more thing, Dumbass," said another, "I double dare you."

That's when it struck me like a gale force wind. I won't be in here forever. I thought it prudent that 'I check myself before I wreck myself'. This is a common prison catch phrase. A thing I should heed, lest I bleed. Their whining put a damper on my euphoria. This is just the sort of unwelcome nuisance that colors the mental outlook a misty bleak.

Have you ever noticed how haters insist on spewing venom on your dreams? Theirs is an attempt to steal your mojo, erase your cool, and throw out the leg to trip you up. They lurk about spitting on their hands determined to ruin your whole life's happiness.

What's up with all the scorn anyway? I was in excellent voice. I sang high. I sang low. I can't remember when I sounded so gosh darn good. It was a performance, which should've received more than a word of grateful appreciation. Who knew so many felons were tone deaf?

I nursed my strained vocal cords in an offended quiet. That's when my conscience gave me a poke in the ribs. My better-self decided to weigh in. Sure, they were horrid people, but this doesn't relieve me of my responsibility to illustrate a sweeter, kinder view of life. Puny and simple as their lives were, it did seem to resemble my own at present.

Gripped by this nobler thought, I acquiesced and offered a conciliatory, "I'm sorry." I searched my thoughts for a more weighty comment but found nothing.

As it was my civil duty, I put myself on mute confining a cheerful, uplifting melody to my heads interior. In no time, I was feeling chipper than whatnot once more. I reminded myself that although the ordeal may have been disagreeable to my audience, a good time was had by me.

FOURTEEN

Teri is twenty-four, a white girl of average height, packing an extra fifteen pounds. She has long black wavy hair and a face that's easy to look at but not necessarily pretty. She's my new bunky. Her being in the hole is, as she puts it, "a total misunderstanding." Teri is a victim of circumstance. Turns out this jail is crawling with misapprehended injured parties. Lots of people in jail have been framed.

First impression might lead one to believe that Teri is a nice, easygoing kind of gal. I wasn't taken unawares by her casual outer shell. Psychopaths are always charming and congenial. Remember Ted Bundy? He was as nice as pie and played a mean game of tennis.

These predators are often disguised as the jerk-off next store wearing the easily forgotten appearance of old so-and-so and what's their face. One mustn't be caught off-guard by the mundane. These fraudsters are as nice as they can be, just the picture of well-adjusted, right up to the time that they are tossing your severed body parts into a roaring incinerator.

Teri told me she signed a plea for one year flat-time. While serving a flat-time sentence the prisoner isn't eligible for release on any basis until they has served the entire sentence imposed by the court.

Teri was arrested on charges of assault with a deadly weapon. She explained that her lesbian lover called the police after Teri stabbed her "just" a couple times with a serrated steak knife. Teri said she would've called the police herself, "because I was so damned mad at that bitch, but I didn't know the number for 911."

I couldn't help but take this as a sign. Not having the heart to tell her, I simply shrugged in a noncommittal gesture as if to suggest that such a thing was impossible for anyone to know.

Teri stabbed her domestic partner once in the shoulder and then twice in the back of the head.

That head thing happens whenever they try to get away. Clearly, the girl was asking for it. In keeping with the Universal Standard Lesbian Codes of Conduct, because the girlfriend didn't die, the girlfriend didn't press charges. County jail administrators, who are interested in generating revenue, thoughtfully picked up the charges. Jails are funded, courtesy of other people's money, per fish they hook. Playing catch and release isn't in the game plan. Even if you aren't guilty as charged, surely you're guilty of something. They will pull out your teeth, one by one, until you come clean with it.

Teri described her particular incident as "a silly little domestic squabble, which happened to include severed flesh and a trip to emergency."

I presented an expression that I hoped communicated that these things happen to the best of us.

"Do you have any priors, Teri?" I asked.

"No," she said then hesitated. "Not unless you count that attempted murder charge at the age of sixteen. I was just a minor."

HOLY MACKEREL! I'm trapped in tight quarters with Charles Manson's daughter. It is just she, I, and no eyewitness. It was, in retrospect, a ritual jamboree in one cell of victim and suspect, a staged preliminary to murder.

You and I can effortlessly deduce that if there are two people in a locked room and one ends up dead, the one still breathing becomes a prime suspect. The trouble is Teri isn't burdened by intelligence.

"Well, some might view a previous conviction as a prior but not me!" I said hoping to seem agreeable.

Teri was happy to explain the circumstances leading up to her previous but not necessarily prior conviction.

Teri described her stepmother as a meddling blabbermouth.

"She thought she was the boss of me." Teri said glaring wild-eyed at the floor. "Something had to be done with her."

An adolescent Teri was certain that a solution to all her troubles lie just under the kitchen sink. She examined the warning labels on the poisonous cleaning supplies. After careful consideration, she decided to bleach her annoying stepmother to death. She poured the chlorine-based liquid whitening agent into a pitcher of lemonade. For good measure, she also added a little bleach to a tray of ice cubes.

Bleach smells awful, tastes awful (I'm guessing here), and would send all kinds of chemical warning signals to the would-be target. I'm thinking that Antifreeze would've been the better way to go. Mercury poisoning is the other feasible option. But no, bleach it was.

It came as no big surprise that when Teri served up one Clorox cocktail, shaken not stirred, suspicions were overexcited. Alerted by the noxious smell, stepmother didn't imbibe the lethal concoction. Instead, she called the police.

Teri lived in a small midwestern town. This dirty deed made her a local celebrity of sorts. She was delighted by her ill-gotten reputation.

"I was something of a big deal in that backwater town." Teri said with hands on hips. She was nodding approvingly at this accomplishment.

I searched her face for the slightest sign of remorse and found nothing.

Teri was remanded to juvenile detention where she stayed for two years. At the age of eighteen, she was released back out into the general population where she would be free to attempt murder once more.

+++

Day three into this disagreeable cellmate arrangement, Teri and I discover that we couldn't stand one another. We were like two negative ends of a magnet repelling each other in accordance with some irrefutable law of nature. Ours was a hate that there was no cure for. An extreme dislike we women can justify by mere consideration.

I don't like her, and what a bitch, is just a small sampling of word pairings, which become the seeds that can sprout extreme loathing. We detested each other fiercely for hundreds of reasons, none of which we could actually put into words. It was more than a feeling and as tangible as an impacted colon.

Teri had developed into something of a nuisance. Her company left me wanting to drown myself in the commode. In fact, if she were drowning I'd gladly toss her an anchor.

I had fulfilled twenty of my thirty-day obligation in segregation. During this time, I've had cellmates who have come and gone. Teri wasn't going anywhere. I did not intend to spend the remaining ten days in purgatory with the likes of her. Something had to be done.

I had a great idea. Granted, I do have a long history of "great idea's" that mostly got me into big trouble. However, this one I felt pretty darn good about. I examined my reckless intentions narrowly at every angle and couldn't see where it could possibly fail. I planned to get under Teri's skin. I intend to wear her down to such a degree that she'll beg to be moved to another cell.

I was thrilled by the prospect of having something to do. This could be an opportunity for bona fide fun in the screwing with someone's head department.

I realize I've vowed earlier to turn a new leaf, change my contemptuous ways. I'm afraid these noble intentions must be slid to the back burner.

I feel my better-self shaking its head in abject disappointment.

Okay, all right, fine. Because I don't have my Magic 8-Ball handy, we will let the Bible decide. I do this often to assist me in major life decisions. I close my eyes, open the Bible to some random page, and place my finger wherever the universe wills it to land. Voila, instant divine direction.

I open my eyes to find myself in the Book of Leviticus. My finger is resting on chapter 19, verse 17, I read, "You shall not hate your sister in your heart but you shall reason frankly with your neighbor, lest you incur sin because of her."

This is a little spooky. I pause for a moment in confusion wondering if this is an enormous coincidence or the setup for a test that I'm sure to fail.

Well, okay. In the interest of fairness, I'll ask myself the following questions: Given the choice, would I rather be kind or right? Which do I think would create a better world?

Hmmm, now let me think. Well, the world is a better place when I'm happy. I'm happiest when I'm right. So, with a clear conscience, I press onward like a wayward Christian soldier.

I started doing little maddening things that, when confronted, I'd vehemently deny. When Teri was let out of the cell to shower, I'd leave obvious clues of my rummaging through her things. Her personal effects would mysteriously come up missing.

"What happen to my Chick-O-Stick?" she whined. "I had two of them and now I only have one."

And tomorrow you'll have none, is what I wanted to say. Instead I said, "I couldn't say, but I'd be happy to help you look for it."

While Teri tried to sleep, I'd pray often and loudly for the salvation of her miserable soul. I'd lie on my bunk alert to all the signs displayed by one who has just successfully dropped off to sleep. I look down below at her bunk. Her mouth was agape, eyes shifting below the lids, drool flowing like a river, and I had to endure the occasional snort.

There is no time like the present I encourage myself. I began prophesying loud enough to rattle the dead. I shared with her my adulterated version of the sinner's prayer.

"God, I know that Teri is a sinner of the most revolting and contemptuous order. I know that she deserves the consequences of her loathsome transgressions. Jesus died and rose again so that this homicidal maniac can be forgiven. Repent you deranged abomination for the Kingdom of Heaven is at hand. Amen and Amen!"

Jarred from a restful sleep, Teri sat up with a start. She let out a pitiful moan that was just dripping with self-pity.

"You jackass!" she screamed. "Do you know that I've just managed to fall asleep?"

"And now you're awake," I point out. "There will be plenty of time for sleep when you're dead. It is later than you think."

Teri grumbles dishing out a handful of the obligatory curse words.

"You may wish to think of me like the Salvation Army, Teri. Before you get the free soup, in your case a little sleep, you'll have to listen to the sermon. As a Christian woman I have an obligation to warn you of certain peril."

"Screw you." Teri twists around in her bed sheet trying to get comfortable. Too bad she doesn't have a pillow to put over her fat head.

"Chances are, Teri, you'll be hurled howling into the lake of fire. Have you ever been eaten alive by flames?" I paused here for effect. Teri grunts in resentment.

"Teri, did you know that the devil was once a radiant and powerful angel? Do you know why he got the boot?" I peek over the edge of my bunk and looked down at her. "Care to venture a guess?"

Teri looked at me with hollow eyes, sneered, and shot me the bird.

I rolled on my back. "Nope," I said to the ceiling cheerfully. "Not even close. Theologians believe that it was the sin of pride. Yep, the pesky old sin of pride. The stuff you're bloated to the gills with. You're puffed up with your own vulgar self-importance. It is a hard thing for the casual observer to stomach. The ruler of the Universe, your Maker, requests that you, a creature of clay, keep his laws and love him. But NO, you won't. You shake a defiant fist to the heavens and holler, no can do mister man, go pound sand."

"Would you please shut the hell up?" Teri pleaded.

I pretend not to hear her.

"God tends to take a dim view of this noncompliant posture. It is this prevailing ungrateful attitude that will one day reduce you to rubble. We're to be like innocent children who wouldn't harm a fly, let alone bump off our dearly beloved Mother."

"Stepmother," Teri screeched in blameless indignation.

Every sin has its justification in the mind of a sinner. Teri kicked the center of my mattress then yelped. I'm guessing the medal platform got the worst of it.

"It's possible that souls are quashed in tough cases such as your own, Teri. Unredeemable, voided, stamped "REJECT" by some bureaucrat in the administrative hub of heaven. You might arrive at the gateway to Heaven already at the wrong address before you're able to honor Saint Peter with your catalogue of excuses."

Teri gave me a bitter, dismissive sniff and screamed stridently.

"Go to Hell!"

My work here is done for the time being. Gratified by her discontent, I breathe in a deep sigh of satisfaction and drifted off into a heavenly slumber.

+++

When Teri woke the next morning, her toothbrush was floating in the toilet. As she gazed into the commode, I could swear I saw a puff of smoke escaping from her ears. Her body stiffened and began to shake some. Her forehead was scrunched up and the lips were pressed together into a tight thin line. Not a good look for her. Her unhappiness brought me delight. She looked into the pooper, then up at me, then down at the floater again, and then at me.

"Tough luck. Into each life some rain must fall."

"Did you throw my toothbrush in the toilet?" Teri seethed with hands on hips.

"Well I'd never!" I give her my injured look.

"Your baseless accusation stings, My Little Sister."

"The hell you wouldn't and don't call me sister!"

Teri scrunched her face to ugly. She gave me the stink-eye.

It was hardly an encouraging start, but I tried again.

"I have been accused of a good many things in my time, notably during police interrogations, but never of an infantile act such as this. I take offense. You have hurt me deeply."

For several seconds Teri and I stared at one another unblinking. Time stood still. By all the laws of good manners, I should say something constructive. As a courtesy, I broke down and confessed my misdeed. I figured it was only a matter of time before she figures out that I was the only other person in the room.

"Okay, okay I surrender." I say with both hands high in the sky. "You caught me dead to rights. I did toss your toothbrush into the shitter."

"What's your problem?" Teri was staring down at the toothbrush not sure if she should flush it or pluck it out.

"I dropped it in there for your own good."

123

Teri's beady eyes were twin dots of contempt.

"I can't be one-hundred percent certain," I said. "But, I've reason to believe that the bristly portion of said poopbrush may have been up my rear end. I must own up to the fact that it brought joy to my heart to watch you brush your teeth yesterday. Regrettably, my better-self insisted on intervening. It can be such a party pooper."

Flames shot from Teri's eye sockets. The woman was remarkably agitated. We sat there staring at each other, two gunslingers, each waiting for the other to make a move.

"I've got three things to say to you, Doughy. Firstly, you're the sickest most disturbed woman I've ever met. Secondly, I'll write this up and bring it to the attention of the next guard on rounds, and thirdly, I intend to take legal action against you. You'll be hearing from my lawyer. You're going to be soooo sorry for this. I hope I've made myself crystal clear, Doughy!"

She finished red faced and resolute.

"Oh, I think so." I said with a yawn. Ticking each point off with my fingers I said, "I'm a sick and disturbed woman, you intend to write this up and bring it to the attention of the next guard on rounds, and you're going to initiate legal proceedings against me. Yep, that makes three all right. So, now that this is out of the way, what do you say we kiss and make up?"

Teri glared, her eyes fixed on me like a rag on a hook.

"Relax, I was just kidding. While incarcerated I've taken a vow of celibacy," I admitted with a shy smile.

"It may shock you to discover, Teri, some people live with moral codes and ethics. No doubt, you would have sex with anything with a pulse. Even without a pulse, you might only require the body still be warm. I, on the other hand, am a high-minded woman of elevated principles and purpose. Sure, I do have a tendency to steal anything that isn't securely anchored to a floorboard. This foible aside, I'm a model of all the other virtues. I intend to stand firm on my commitment to chastity even if my private parts catch on fire."

Teri grimaced in disgust.

"You really are very uptight. I've yet to detect the slightest hint of a sense of humor in your personality. It is well known that humor affords us an aloofness and ability to rise above difficult situations and people like you. You know, Miss Dreary, humor is said to be another of the soul's weapons in the fight for self-preservation. True enough, your destitute soul is minuscule, if it exists at all. This is regrettable when one considers that our soul is the only thing we have that God will measure. Still, one should try to remain encouraged."

It pains me to report that my goodwill and chipper words of propping-up fell on wax laden ears once more. Teri responded with a sneer. Then she suggested I do something in the way of fornicating myself.

Teri lodged numerous complaints. Surprisingly, I never heard from that lawyer of hers. When a guard pressed me for an explanation, I executed the universal crazy sign, spinning an index finger in a circular motion to the right of my temple. This was accompanied by an earnest shrug and wide-eyed look of astonishment.

"We all know perfectly well, although she won't admit it, that Teri is a raving lunatic." I explain to the guard's vacant face. "All her blather is the product of an infected imagination. The medication she takes alters her perception of reality."

"This one's on meds?"

"Bucket's full of them, difficult upbringing you know. It's rather a gloomy state of affairs." I say with pursed lips and a sad shake of the head.

The guard stares at me, her face, like some foreign language, indecipherable.

"She shoved my toothbrush up her ass." Teri screamed red faced with disgust.

The officer wrinkles the forehead. She looks at Teri then back at me.

I give her my isn't-it-sad look and nod the head as if the whole situation pained me.

"It really is too bad. Still, that's life isn't it? The poor thing's a train wreck and the rest of us are duty-bound to muddle through the fallout. 'We then that are strong ought to bear the infirmities of the weak, and not to please ourselves.' That's right out of the Book of Romans."

"Is that right?"

The officer wasn't moved.

"You probably see this sort of thing all the time, Officer. What can you do? The thing is just too sad for words." I press the eye as if to prevent a tear from falling.

The guard eyes me doubtfully. Frowning with uncertainty, she heaves a heavy sigh and moves on toward her next source of aggravation.

I know I'm dead wrong and in all probability creating yet another rung to my ladder to hell. My level of immaturity is staggering. My body has always been more grownup than my brain. If maturity was measured in height, I'd be a midget.

Teri had reached her snapping point when she discovered that I had torn out and flushed the last chapter of a paperback that she was totally engrossed in. It was a real page-turner that I had read and shared with her in the guise of sisterhood.

It was John Saul's, "Punish the Sinners": Is hysteria manipulating these innocent children into violent self-destruction? Or has a supernatural force, thirteenth-century madness, returned to...Punish the Sinners. Oooh! Aaaahhh! Unbeknownst to Teri, she'll never find out.

She was gripped beyond my wildest dreams. Teri didn't so much read but guzzle the medieval tale of terror. Her face was crimson with excitement, her eyes bulged, and breath quickened. She was captivated. It was as if she had found writing suited to her intellectual powers and it felt so right.

I waited with baited breath for her to reach her last page. I was eager to reap what I had painstakingly sown.

Teri let out a passionate cry like that of a mother watching a Dingo eat her baby. In a hysterical frenzy, she leaped from the bottom bunk. The way she came out of that bed, you would've thought a red-hot poker came up through her mattress. I sensed it must be show time. Her face was a fire engine red and she was foaming at the mouth. I was reminded of my very first rabies vaccination. I half expected to see Teri bark and bite at the air.

"Are you okay?" I asked jumping down from my bunk. I placed a concerned hand on her shoulder and leaned forward in a display of deep alarm.

"You know, I couldn't help but notice you have anger management issues. Impatience is your constant companion. Anger is a dreadful disease that kills," I counsel. "The slightest disruption infuriates you. Do you realize that your fury against people and circumstances only aggravate your sickness? You would do well to avoid paying attention to every unpleasantness that comes down the pike."

My guidance seemed to result in a bit of a lull in the proceedings. For about four and a half seconds or possibly longer, we just stood there drinking each other in. The unspoken challenge hung like a cloud above our heads. Our staring contest produced a tension that Teri could no longer stand. She screwed up her face making it ugly then turned her gaze to the floor.

"I win," I holler in the same passionate tone I use when I win at bingo.

Her teeth were clinched and her soulless eyes were boring a hole into the grey cement floor. The poor thing has so many problems and now I learn that she's the sorest loser on the planet too.

For a full week, Teri had been enduring my exploits. The strain had taken its toll. Little by little, day-by-day, she was slowly turning into a human volcano. This final outrage blew the lid off her. For a long moment, it seemed Teri, her feeble strength taxed beyond its limit of endurance, was about to suffer something in the nature of spontaneous combustion. This was precisely the kind of bazaar state of affairs that cheers me up.

"I've had it with you, Doughy," is the only thing she said that I can repeat. Suffice it to say, this young lady needs her mouth washed out with Sodium Cyanide. Teri is obviously the product of parents who opted to spare the rod.

Completely out of her mind, Teri held the defunct paperback in one hand; the other hand was in a fist, knuckles white, waving both appendages wildly, high in the sky. In all affairs of human tension there must come a breaking point.

In a rage, she slams the paperback against the wall and lunged at me. She wrapped her fingers around my delicate neck.

If I didn't know any better, I'd say she wanted me dead. No worries. Teri's angry shrills had alerted the guards to a possible disturbance. I could hear several sets of military style boots en route. In a matter a minutes this bloodthirsty killer would no longer be my problem.

Just in the nick of time, four officers barged into our cell armed with pepper spray and tazor guns. They removed Teri from my throat and then from the cell.

Because I appeared to still be breathing, no one asked me if I was alright. I still think it would've been a nice gesture. Another glaring example of how common courtesy is just not so common anymore.

As I've never been one to concern myself with lawsuits or litigation, I won't be pressing charges. However, Teri is still in big trouble. She was caught red-handed strangling a fellow inmate. This isn't good. I see a brand spanking new aggravated assault charge in her extreme near future. She's going to get a page-two.

This means that Teri will be taken downtown and processed in on new charges. Not fun! Oh my, that's too bad. Murderous proclivity aside, Teri seemed like a real nice girl.

FIFTEEN

I've done my time in the hole. I'm back in tent city. The hole serves as a capital attitude adjuster. I decided to settle into a more-or-less trouble free rapport with these bureaucratic bullies. I may even be on my best behavior, within reason.

Dinner tray in hand, I look around the dayroom for a seat. The place is packed. There are more female inmates than there are seats and many are sitting on the floor. I spied a vacancy. With a series of excuse me, pardon me's, I make my way toward the empty bench space. What a lucky break. I placed my tray on the table. Chow was first-rate: a hot pocket, green beans, applesauce, and a brownie.

I couldn't help but notice that things got real quiet when I sat down. The air at this table was stifling. The girls were pretending not to look at me, peering slyly over their trays. I smiled affably but said nothing. I had a sneaking suspicion that I've blundered into well-marked territory.

Midway through a bite of applesauce, I sense a hovering presence. I looked to my right and upward. There stood a scrawny Mexican chick without a hint of a soul glaring down at me with eyes as sinister as the Republican Party. The air around her was charged with hostility. Her manner screamed troubled childhood. She had long black hair tightly braided, her face was the color of a dirty pillowcase, and her black beady eyes were filled with malicious intent.

"Yooo, this table is for La Raza."

With a closed fist, she pounds her chest.

"White bitches sit over there."

With a host of hate in her eyes, she pointed to a table full of faces a lighter shade of pale.

Over the past eight months, I've become skilled at smiling and nodding at the most outrageous stupidity. I've developed a great

129

appetite for the absurd. I've been toughened and fortified by the routine of one-damn-thing-after-another which constitutes life in this lunatic asylum.

I was preparing to turn the other cheek. Nelson Mandela said, "Forgiveness liberates the soul. It removes fear. That's why it is such a powerful weapon."

"No place to sit." I said.

With calm resolve, I slide a plastic spoon into my applesauce.

"That's too f#@# bad for you, Puta."

She bent in closer to suggest she was serious. She looked like the type that might carry a shiv. I checked her hands. Who was Puta?

"Who?" I asked.

She must have me mixed up with someone else.

"Puta." Scrawny spewed, spraying a gob of spittle that landed smack-dab in the middle of my applesauce.

"Yuck, what the hell?"

This sort of thing cannot be overlooked. That applesauce was very tastee. Before I could turn and rebuke this interloper for polluting my foodies, she placed her hand on my right shoulder. She gathered a fist full of my shirt in her rodent paw.

I cringe. Now this nuisance has gone too far. I could squash this pipsqueak into mincemeat. I remind myself not to overreact. I don't want to go back to the hole. I turned and gave Scrawny a look sharp enough to circumcise.

"Back Off!"

A guard approached our table.

"Is there a problem here, Ladies?"

Letting go of my shirt, Scrawny hastily scurried off like a cockroach to lights on.

"No, Officer, everything is fine."

With a look of suspicion, the officer hesitated. Then she moved on.

"Good for you," said a quiet voice from across the table.

I looked up and met the woman's nervous brown eyes. She gave a curt nod then quickly diverted her gaze back down to her food.

"Yes," said a woman to my left. She spoke in a whisper and didn't look in my direction.

I said nothing.

I looked down at my tray in disappointment. The thought of flying discharge made me want to heave. I picked up the tray intent to dump the contents and add it to the stack of empties.

"Hey, are you going to finish that?" asked a well-fed face.

"No."

I put the tray back on the table and headed to the yard.

As was my routine, after chow I walked briskly for forty minutes. Today I walked with some trepidation. What was started at chow wasn't finished. I suppose that you can't be in jail and not hit turbulence.

My only plan was to keep my knowledge and worries to myself. It is possible that I'm being deceived by my own fears, or I'm in a crisis. If the latter is true, I needed calm and clear thinking. Bionic powers and the ability to take flight would be an enormous benefit as well. For good measure, I supplemented my walk with a couple of Our Father's.

On round two of my circle about the encampment, I ran into Scrawny accompanied by two bulky Latino sidekicks. I didn't stop walking. After passing and on second thought, I stopped. I turned and called back to them.

"If you have something to say, you'll have to walk and talk."

Scrawny and her goons caught up.

"You can't disrespect La Raza like that," Scrawny said. This time she did not pound her chest like a primate. I was a little disappointed.

"Oh, I see." I said, but I really didn't.

"You have to apologize or you have to fight."

"I don't have any idea what you're talking about. I've done nothing to apologize for and I've no reason to fight anyone. We're going to have to pick up the pace. You ladies are welcome to join me. This conversation is over."

I quicken my cadence. They didn't follow. They stopped in their tracks, no doubt chastising my departing backside.

That went well I thought, forcing optimism. Making my final rotation around the yard, I had a vague sense that things were about to go very wrong.

The two goons approached me from behind. The big one grabbed my right arm; the bigger one gripped my left. I was lifted and moved, my toes tapping the gravel. They brought me to a section of the yard that was a known blind spot to surveillance cameras.

I found myself standing in front of a beast of a woman. There is indeed a "missing link" and I'm certain I've just found her. All together, this isn't a satisfactory turn of events.

"Apologize," the Beast snarled.

Heart in mouth, I said, "NO".

My tone stunk of desperation. I was scared, bluffing with a poker face that betrayed me. I felt like a woman on a powder keg with the burning fuse close to blastoff.

The Beast couldn't let such impertinence go unchallenged. It would look weak.

Nothing in my life had prepared me for this particular moment. What in the hell is the matter with me? I wonder. Have I lost my mind? I mean to say, I'm not afraid to die, but I'm thinking that this is really going to hurt. For the love of God, what have I gotten myself into?

I received an instant message in the form of a sharp blow to the left side of my head. This colossus put me out of commission with one hand. Now might be a good time to call a priest.

I'd later learn that I had been clobbered with a sock full of wrought-steel combination locks. They call this pummeling device a "slock". I call it very bad manners. The locks, for your slock, can be purchased through the commissary for eight dollars and were used to secure a 12 X 12 X 12 inch deep locker issued to each inmate. The lockers, located in the dayroom, were used to store hygiene products and doubled as a mailbox for incoming post. Livings among thieves made the lock purchase a necessity.

My heart was pounding in surprise and panic. I reel back a step under the impact of the blow, the force of it left me disoriented and unsteady, but I didn't fall. I stumbled backwards three more steps and found my back against a chain link fence. I looked down at the gravel ground cover, saw fresh bright drops of something dark red, and wondered if they came from me. I felt a warm thick liquid flow down the side of my face and neck. I detected a sharp metallic scent.

I clamp my left hand to my head with a grimace. My hair is plastered to my skull, sticky and wet. I looked at my bloody hand. Holy shit! My stomach turned to water and I nearly throw up.

Using my hands as support, I walked myself down the fence until I was in a sitting position, my legs jetting out in front of me. I felt the world around me suddenly begin to narrow. I closed my eyes briefly and said a silent prayer.

"Lord, I'm scared. Don't let me pass-out and please send an Angel. Amen."

My head didn't hurt. The blood was flowing in sheets. I knew I had to apply pressure to stop the bleeding. I lifted my hand off the gravel, but only managed to move it six inches off the ground. Unable to gather the strength to lift it higher, I let it drop. I broke out in a cold sweat. I started seeing sparkly lights and black dots before my eyes. I couldn't move.

The good news was that my bowels were working just fine and had proceeded directly into emergency evacuation mode.

The only thing more embarrassing then pooping your pants in public is doing so in front of a live audience. This detail was too intense to face without mortification. The smell and the squashy wetness... I don't want to think about it. Now would be a good time to die. I began to wonder if passing out was actually the better way to go. It didn't look like that was going to happen. With the elimination of surplus toxins from my system, I slowly began to feel better. A small crowd had developed. All eyes, much to my discomfort, were turned in my direction.

Inmates stepped aside deferentially as Camilla pushed her way through the mob. Camilla was a distinguished woman with kind intelligent eyes. Too big in the hips, I heard the other girls say, but I didn't think so.

Camilla looked down at me. Then she looked up at the Beast who she spoke sharply to. In a matter of moments, she reduced this ferocious grizzly to a timid domestic pet. The Beast, behaving like a scolded child, lowered her head and sulked.

Camilla knelt down in front of me. I watched a tear tumble down her cheek. The love in her face was so real that it made me want to cry.

"Are you ok?" She asked.

I thanked God for sending her. I felt the tears rising to my eyes. I breathed in deep and willed them back.

"I think I'm okay, but..." I pause. This is embarrassing. Timidly and in a murmur I say, "I had an accident in my pants."

This made her smile showing teeth very white and even. She was prettier than she intended to appear.

"That's okay. Everything is going to be just fine."

Camilla's voice was calming and competent. A moisturizing balm formulated to take away the pain and humiliation of what had just happened.

A woman handed Camilla a towel. Camilla balled up one half of the towel and pressed it against the top left side of my head. With the other half of the towel, she wiped the blood off my face and neck. It seemed the kindest gesture that anyone had ever shown me, anyone at all. A second towel was used to put over my shoulders to cover my blood stained shirt.

"Can you walk?" Camilla asked.

"Yes."

We had to walk from the far corner of the yard to the open bay showers located in the dayroom. Doing so without being detected by a guard required a group effort. In here, the law punishes the masses for the wrong doing of one. If a guard sees blood, they start asking questions. I fell off my bunk is the standard go to response but is rarely well received. The injured is sent to medical for repairs and if they don't tattle they end up in the hole. If they do tattle they end up in the hole segregated for their own safety. Meanwhile, the entire compound goes into lockdown until a satisfactory explanation materializes.

These women are all seasoned barometers fine-tuned to detect the slightest change in the political and communal atmosphere. When it comes to prison authorities, there is a pervasive "them against us" mentality. We don't trust or like them and will protect each other. We will put aside all pride and prejudice, instinctively and in an instant. A classic example of how friendships are forged in alliance against a common enemy.

In an extraordinary display of interracial solidarity, I'm methodically moved toward the desire destination. We travel in a group of four passing lookout's posted to alert us of guard sightings. "Twenty-two" is a term that often traveled from tent to tent. It is meant to alert unsuspecting, smoking, and fornicating convicts that there is a cop on the yard and en route. The code word originated from the slang term "five" "Oh", which is code for a cop on the outs. A guard is considered less than half a cop. Therefore, fifty divided by two minus three, for good measure, gives you twenty-two.

+++

When we reached the shower bay, it's empty. This wasn't accidental. On a plastic scoop chair was a clean set of stripes, undies, soap, shampoo and fresh towels. This is why I love women.

Two girls casually stood guard outside of the shower to keep others out. One of the girls told me to take all the time I needed. We were as thick as thieves. Then too, if thieves were so thick plea bargains would not be so popular.

Standing under the spray, my eyes were fixed on the red water making its way to the drain. It brought me right back to the shower I took right after the rape. I was thirteen. I remember seeing the same diluted blood rushing toward a silver ring that led to the public sewage system. This fresh new indignity, like the unwanted sex, will have to be kept secret and added to my list of things that I have to pretend never happened.

All this thinking is making my head throb.

+++

My wrongdoing was obviously more serious than I had realized. I'd later learn from Camilla some of the rules that dictate inmate's behavior here in the tents. These rules didn't seem to apply to inside lockup, insofar as I could tell.

The tent city inmates have in place subcultures that divide the great unwashed by skin tone. Each race has a cluster of counsel persons appointed to run the show for their peeps.

They are divided into four categories: Kinfolk are Blacks, La Raza is Hispanics, The Woods are Whites, and Natives are Indians.

Those who fall neatly into one of the relevant categories can enjoy the benefits of a support system that includes: a head, assistant head, mail person, and a torpedo.

The heads are in place to keep the peace among their tribe. They also decide who lives and dies.

The assistant head, I suppose this one is apparent.

The mail person doesn't handle the mail your Mommy sends, but internal and unauthorized pieces of parcel referred to as kites. Kites are letters that are folded like a paper football. They are used to communicate with unsentenced females located inside, as well as the boys on the other side of the fence.

A fist full of kites are stuffed into a pink sock and lobbed over the fence to the men's side at the exact same time, twice daily. Mail persons on both sides of the fence coordinate the exchange. Many a love connection has been inspired through this underground postal service, making it exactly like Internet dating, except for the differences. More commonly, women are requesting tobacco with the promise of sexual favors upon release.

What in the hell is a torpedo? A torpedo is a manly brute of a woman. She is a female "Stone Cold", Steve Austin, only stockier with more facial hair and a mullet. A torpedo is assigned the task of pulverizing and disfiguring anyone not of like skin tone who might be dissing their peeps. Be it real or imagined they make no distinction.

136

Camilla's explanation brought clarity to my latest fresh new indignity. With Camilla as my protector, I was now, essentially, Hispanic. Not only was I permitted to sit at the La Raza's table, Camilla insisted on it. This was very good of her. However, I was secretly hoping to become Black.

SIXTEEN

Whether you're living indoors or outdoors here at ItsHella County Jail, entertainment is plentiful. There are more characters housed in this compound then you'll find at Universal Studios. For those who pray well with others, a Bible study can be soul stirring and spiritually thought provoking. The White and Latino gatherings are normally tame. The Blacks, on the other hand, praise God with a vengeance. They are over-the-top breathing hellfire and damnation. It is a thing not to be missed.

"Crack is the blood of Satan, liquor is his breath, and fornication his delight." shrilled my black sister handling a Bible. Formally, she had handled many a penis, which landed her in the pokey for the sixth time.

Sharon was fortyish. She had a discount rate whores tough, more handsome than pretty face. The thing you notice first about Sharon is that her skin is very dark like the color of a Hersey bar. The second thing that you may find riveting is how her cheeks are deeply potholed. The unsightly gouges in her face, looks for all the world, like somebody came at her with the sizzling end of a cigar at some point in her career path. I managed to ignore the knowledge of her former life skills and potential horrors. Instead, I focused on her message.

"Wicked Sinners," roared the mouthpiece of heaven. Her vocal vibrations rattled the tent flaps.

"You're the product of accidental pregnancies, the result of stupid choices, misbegotten souvenirs of rape, promiscuity, desire, and too much drink. YOU'RE the consequence of lusting, pulsating flesh lost in its own vile pleasures. AND here you sit doomed to repeat the misery from which you came. Look into the faces of your fallen sisters conceived in selfish desire and filled with evil doing. Are you guilty of trafficking with Satan?" She bellows slamming an overused Bible to her knees.

We all hung our heads in shame.

It seemed like a loaded question under the circumstances. No offense, but Sharon is a harlot, a regular Mary Magdalene, selling her favors to the lowest common denominator. The great whore who corrupts the Earth with fornication, or so the scripture's put it. How dare she slam an accusatory bible at us? This two-bit whore has some nerve. Yet, I found her oddly compelling. I was eager to hear more.

"Jesus frees us, My Nigger's." She shrieked with evangelical zeal. Although my nickname to this group was Casper and sometimes Two-Ply, I knew she was talking directly to me.

"When two or more gather in his name, he will make his presence known." She roared.

And then it appeared. A miracle in the form of a portly green baloney fed pigeon. In it flew, relieving itself on the concrete slab floor of our expired dairy scented tent. As we all gazed into the deposit, we saw it, clear as day. If you held your head just right then slightly left sort of, you could see the Virgin Mary holding up a sign that read "No MSG."

After a short brainstorming assemblage, the group concluded that the Virgin Mother was telling us she had "No Message" or "To steer clear of chow mein".

Ah, sweet mysteries of life. I've come to expect such miracles in Tent City. Because such marvels are commonplace, this one was short lived. The thundering sermon continued.

"Get on your knees sinners and tremble before the might of Jehovah!"

All knees hit the concrete slab.

Sharon flipped to the Book of Job and began to paraphrase loosely. "The triumphing of the wicked is squat and the joy of the vile hypocrite is shorter than the time it takes to turn a trick. You sinners will all perish forever like your own dung. You'll burn eternally in Hell lost in eternal damnation forever because Lucifer's coming to get Y.O.U!"

Compunction worked strongly in the audience. There were groans and weeping.

I was trembling and wet my pants, just a little. My heart was pounding in my chest and I was overcome with alarm.

Oh sweet horror! I was looking around wildly. In a panic, I latched on to the metal leg of the nearest bunk in hopes that Lucifer would not take me.

Fellow worshipers worked together to pry my frantic fingers from the metal peg leg.

"Satan was probably too busy to stop by today," Tasheka said softly.

"It's gonna be okay now." Another woman assured me.

The soothing words were like balm to my frazzled nerves. I felt a sense of camaraderie and fellowship that warmed the cockles of my heart.

In that instant, I felt washed in the presence of the Holy Ghost. Hope strung eternal in my bosom. This jubilance, the joy in my spirit caused an urgent need to spread the good news. "Jesus frees us, My Niggers." I ejaculate.

My little light was blazing bright. I was beaming with a full-blown chimpanzee grin and my cup runneth over.

That's when I noticed that the rest of the parishioners did not share my high spirits. The tent had suddenly become a chill. Every eye was on me. All were stern and disapproving. Now what did I do? Rather than guess, I came right out with it.

"What?"

"You can't say the "N" word," said a sister incredulously.

"But she did!" I said pointing an accusatory finger at the ringleader.

"Black people can say it all they want, but you can't say it, Cracker."

"Oh," I said. The scales had fallen from my eyes. "I didn't know there were rules about these things."

"Ohhhh, yeah, there are definitely rules," said the women in unison.

"You mean like the way we can piss and moan about the stupidity of our Government, but if a foreigner does the same thing, we get mad?"

The girls talk amongst themselves and collectively shrug.

"Well, not exactly but close enough. We're gonna let you slide this time Two-Ply, since you don't seem to know much about anything."

"Thanks, I think." Relief reshaped my face.

After a group hug we sang, "I want to get to Heaven with my wrong foul breath".

Anywho, that's what I sang. Everyone else was singing, "I want to get to Heaven, my long-sought rest".

+++

There is nothing like a Holy revival to spritz the cobwebs right out of the old weary soul. I was so full of the Holy Spirit. I could burst. I came away from that experience a changed woman. This sort of thing makes a girl hungry. Not for salvation, I was thinking more on the lines of a Chick-O-Stick.

Moving toward the dayroom, I nod cordially to passersby. I was just brisling with the peace that passes all understanding, feeling chipper than whatnot.

"Good morning, Ladies." I beamed.

"I wish you peace like a river and joy like a fountain flows where ever you go."

"What in the hell is her problem?" One of the girls was rude enough to say out loud.

The other girl scrunched her face to ugly and shrugged rather clueless.

Heading toward my assigned locker, I dialed up my secret code and popped open the lock. Pushing aside some hygiene products, I laid an eager hand on the prize.

I found an empty table portion that offered a bird's-eye view of the dayroom and the hustle and bustle there in. Here I enjoyed my snack while participating in my favorite past time, people watching.

I observe girls getting things from their lockers and making their way to the open bay shower that was just at my back. I'm painfully shy when it comes to matters of exposure. Private parts have been so named for a reason. You may be thinking a lesbian must love the prospect of showering with a gaggle of women. Think again. These girls aren't bikini models, more exhibits in a freak show. As for myself, I might qualify as a main attraction. It is my unsolicited opinion that some things should be done in complete and utter isolation.

141

The dayroom has the look of a high school cafeteria in that it contains numerous long tables with attached bench seating. It is about half the size of an auditorium without the high ceilings. This room serves as a social retreat. Some are playing cards, some chatting, and others are eating. There are others, like me, who prefer to be left alone. Popularity never seemed worth the energy required to achieve it.

As I people watch, I notice a couple girls going through the lockers of those who either haven't the means or the good sense to purchase a lock. They are stealing food. No food is permitted to be stored or eaten out in the tents.

Tent city is riddled with such rules all of which, like in tax preparation, one only learns of after you have broken them. Wearisome penalties often follow.

There is a guard bubble in the dayroom. The windows are so dark you can't see inside. So long as you work and behave, they don't bother you so much out here. I only go to the bubble for tank orders and a disposable razor. Razors must be returned within fifteen minutes. Looking toward the guard station, I noticed four newcomers being ushered in and instructed to sit.

That's when I saw her. My heart quickens, a wide smile formed on my face, and involuntarily, I screamed.

"Maria."

She looked my way, as did most everyone present. I was out of my seat and headed her way. She rose to meet me.

We embraced.

"It is so good to see you!" I said.

"And you," Maria said with an affectionate smile. "But what're you doing here?"

"I never left. I got a year in tents. I've six more calendar months left."

"You never left?"

"Nope, what're you doing here?"

Maria bent her eyes to the floor.

"I suppose working as a hotel receptionist wasn't such a good idea. My old johns found out where I was and started coming around. It was impossible to make ends meet on minimum wage."

"Minimum wage is a hard pill to swallow." I say.

"You're not kidding. You certainly can't live on it. Anyway, one thing led to another and well, here I am."

"I understand," I said. "No worries, this place is great."

"Still the human sunbeam, I see." Maria said.

"False illusion and artificial optimism has made me the woman I am today. Like I always say my, Dear Sister, difficulty is inevitable, misery an option."

"I missed you." Maria said.

"I'm really glad to see you. And for reals, compared to indoor lockup, this place is a shut-ins paradise. I promise the time will fly. How long will you be here?"

"They gave me six months."

"Perfect, the first thing you'll need to do is put in a tank order. I want you to volunteer for chain gang duty."

Maria eyed me narrowly.

"It's too hot to be out in the tents right now. Chain gang duty will put you indoors for a month. You'll go on road trips Monday through Friday, and best of all, you'll see me. I'm the trustee."

"You're the trustee for the chain gang?"

"Yes, it is a gravy job. And just wait until the chain gang officers get a load of you. You have capability and aptitude that's impossible to over praise. I'm certain they will permit you to be a trustee after you graduate."

"What do you mean Graduate?"

"Yeah, it's a thirty day program. It will be a cake walk for you."

Maria didn't seem wholly convinced. A couple days in this monsoon season heat should prove more persuasive.

"So," Maria said changing the subject, "how many times have you fallen in love out here?"

"Well," I said with mild indignation. "I'm sure I don't know what you're talking about."

"You fall in love with practically every female you meet and with a dozen you've only seen from a distance?"

"I'm sure you have me mixed up with someone else." I said crossing my arms at the chest and narrowing the eyes.

I forgot how Maria loved to strike at the exposed nerve. She has a knack of knowing exactly what not to say.

I was just about to become more self-protective and tell her how she was prone to exaggeration when Gabriella stepped toward us.

My spine turned to silly putty and parts of my brain began to atrophy. For a split second, I forgot how to breathe. In her presence, I always felt like I'm going under the ether. Gabriella is a pretty girl. She is petite, delicate, and willowy. She walks about with a proud tilt to her head and an energetic step to her gait that spoke of good physical condition.

"Hello," I said with the love light in my eyes.

"There is a card game in the laundry tent in twenty minutes. We're playing for tobacco. Would you be a dear and bring some around?" Gabriella was her charming self, giving me a full dose of fascinating personality.

"Gabriella, this is Maria, a very good friend of mine."

Gabriella turned her attention to Maria. She gave her a hypercritical up and down, followed by a purposely-cruel smile and a throaty, "Hmmm".

I gave Gabriella a penetrating look in an attempt to will her to be nice. My smoke signal went unnoticed.

Turning her attention back to me, Gabriella gave me that flashing smile accompanied by the quick sidelong look.

"Be sure to be there in twenty and try not to disappoint."

"Oh, I won't."

Gabriella turned superciliously and sauntered away.

I sighed deeply and turned to Maria.

"Isn't she just beautiful?"

"Oh boy, beautiful like a nuclear explosion. Fascinating to view from a distance but you don't want to get too close. How long have you been pining over that devastated area?"

144

"She just takes a little getting used to." I said defensively.

"My God, I thought you scraped the bottom of the barrel with Angel, but I see you managed to dig deeper still to extricate that piranha."

It saddens me to report that Maria has not changed one iota. I pretended not to hear her. What I lack in good communication skills, I make up for in being a poor listener.

"When did you start smoking?" Maria asked.

"Oh, I don't smoke but she does so..."

"But of course." Maria interrupted.

"Have you written her one of your sappy poems yet?"

Maria is snickering.

I used this juncture to move head long into my sonnet.

"Behold, thou art fair, my love; behold, thou art fair; thou hast doves' eyes within thy locks: thy hair is as a flock of goats..."

Maria raised a restrictive hand. The color had drained from her face.

"You don't like it? Do you think the goat thing is a bit much? I got that right out of the Bible. Song of Solomon is the Book much loved by the dyed-in-the-wool romantic. It is a highly expressive, rhythmical literary piece that speaks to all the deepest matters of both heart and soul. It makes for a very pleasant read. But," I said confidentially, "don't tell Gabriella where I got it, she's an atheist.

"A Godless woman, say it's not so." Maria says wide-eyed with mock surprise.

"Yes, obviously, this is a matter to impossible to overlook. It will be the first thing I'll need to fix about her. Those who would deny the birthright of their Creator surely condemn their own soul."

"I'd say so."

"Did you know, Maria, atheist haven't one religious holiday?"

"That's fishy."

"Yeah, this aspect alone is all the reason I need not to join. Oh, by the way, did I tell you? Gabriella is an exotic dancer. She has a rare gift. You might think it would make her a stuck-up snob, but NO, not at

145

all. Colossal success has not spoiled her one bit. She's still simple, down to earth, and untouched."

"Is that right? I see she has successfully landed in jail. What did she do?"

Not liking the direction this conversation was going, I took Maria by the arm and proceeded to walk.

"I want you to meet someone," I said. "She's the head of La Raza."

"What's a La Raza?

"I'll explain later."

Camilla was fiddling with her combination lock when we approached. I introduced the two.

Maria extended her hand outward.

Camilla took Maria's hand in both of hers and said with all the enthusiasm of a generous nature, "It is a pleasure to meet you, Maria. I'm on my way to Catholic services. Would you ladies care to join me?"

"Maria is allergic to organized religion," I explained. "I'll take a rain check."

Camilla smiled cordially and was off.

"Camilla is very nice." Maria said. "Why can't you be attracted to a woman like her?"

"Of course I like Camilla, but I'm afraid she's far too good for me. She's a woman of high standards and impeccable moral fiber. Good women are reluctant to put up with any of my crap. You can hardly blame them."

Maria nodded in agreement.

"I'm attracted to her, which is unusual I must say. I rarely notice the nice ones. They can't offer the dysfunction and disturbing neglect I've come to expect from the strangles of a committed relationship."

"That certainly explains your poor choices."

"True enough, I do tend to set the bar low but it's what I'm comfortable with."

Maria's name came over the PA system. She was wanted at the guard station. I walked with her. Maria was getting a bunk assignment. She was going to the welfare tent.

While at the window I asked for a blank tank order and handed it to Maria.

"Volunteer for the chain gang. The timing is perfect. You don't have a job yet. It is too hot to be in the tents. You have options."

Maria took the tank order, but still didn't seem convinced.

+++

During the winter months the mercury falls a little below freezing. In the summer temperatures, exceeding 110 degrees is normal. On these hot days, because heat rises, those who occupy a top bunk can experience midday temperatures of 135 degrees (actual recorded top-bunk temperature mid-July).

The monsoon season is a showcase of dramatic weather. It kicks off in Mid-July and last through to the end of September. Monsoon season brings us high winds, heavy rain, and humidity.

When hell freezes over, we're permitted as many as ten blankets. We sleep in our stripes and several layers of pink long johns.

The sweltering heat offers fewer concessions. Mid day is dreadful. For those who work nights, or like me, six am to noon, the rest of the day is unbearable. The dayroom is hot also. There is a closed seating area for those waiting to be seen for medical, this section is air-conditioned. If you're caught in here trying to cool off, you get run out.

Walking into the showers fully dressed then laying on your bunk offers a temporary reprieve. The key is to drop off to sleep before you're dry. You have ten minutes. You'll wake to find that you feel like someone has set you on fire and then put you out. The puddle you now lay in is a product of your pores and is the temperature of a nice spot of tea.

When conditions become this insufferable, I volunteer for chain gang detail. I've volunteered and have been place on this crew three times. Once to flee solitary confinement and the other times to escape rough weather.

After putting up with two days of sweltering heat, Maria asked me to deliver her tank order to the chain gang officers. I hand carried the document and Maria was assigned to "C" pod the very next day.

147

Chain gang occupies the upstairs tier to one of the solitary confinement pods. As I had predicted the officers loved her. Maria took charge of that group faster than you can say 'who the hell does she think she is?'

The chain gang, whose official name is "The Last Chance Program", is a thirty-day program intended to instill a sense of responsibility and accountability to those of street-thug mentality. Etiquette, protocol, and decorum are drummed into these girls daily. Some volunteer, however eighty percent of the participants are recruited from solitary confinement. The chain gang operates on the premise that discipline and military style scare tactics can transform these bad apples. Sort of like "scared straight" only for these girls, "it's too late".

The chain gang is used mostly for show. Inmates are paraded out into the streets of Phoenixville and the surrounding metropolitan areas. They serve as poster felons for the consequences of bad behavior. A living exhibition of how depraved sinners are treated in these here parts.

The chain gang is a scarlet letter of sorts, shining a brilliant light on those who violate the common law of this police state by way of willful rebellion. Those aberrant wrong doers who drink and drive, smoke the evil marijuana stick, and fornicate for profit will be made an example of by way of public humiliation. There is nothing like a fat dose of penitential self-abasement to set the wayward right.

It is important that we do not lose sight of the fact that this is a county jail, not prison. The majority of the girls here are not murderers. Most are being detained on local misdemeanor charges.

Sherriff Joey Porcupino believes the chain gang to be one of his most ingenious ideas. The average bright eyed, rational American does not trust a politician. Sheriff Porcupino is politics personified. He is clearly unfamiliar, or more likely doesn't care about, international treaties that set human rights standards binding on all United States public servants. Porcupino continues to dazzle Arizonans with his staggering lack of humanity.

He understands that to succeed in affairs of state it is often necessary to rise above ones principles. Old Porcupino is often seen staring vacantly into space reminiscing, in a senile fog, about the good old days when he was just a lad. It was the late eighteen hundreds, an age when the Word of God and the Will of government were one and the same. Porcupino struggles to come to terms with the twenty-first century and its swarms of bleeding heart liberals.

"Left to their devices we'd have peace and harmony among all nations. Bah, Humbug," Porcupino mutters, "that's not the kind of thing that gets votes!"

His formative years were a simpler time when men were men and women were property. Back in his day, evildoers were dealt with severely. It was a straightforward ancient recipe for harshness: an eye for an eye, a tooth for a tooth, an arm and a leg if you're ugly and want sex.

Porcupino can't understand why we did away with the tried and true public lynching. Whose idea was it to stop burning those pesky witches, and hey, what in the heck happened to the guillotine?

Chain gang members are required to work labor detail while in leg chains. There are 15 members, 5 to a chain. As women graduate from the 30-day program, others are yanked from the hole to fill the gaps. Work detail includes roadside cleanup, trash removal, and cemetery maintenance. Additionally, every Thursday we bury the indigent and unclaimed. Not alive, that's on Fridays.

+++

It is eight a.m. Thursday. I place the "Sheriff's Chain Gang at Work" signs on the street just outside the White Flanks Cemetery. This is the counties potter's field. Inside are hundreds of rows of coaster-size brass markers. Each is engraved with a real names or simply, Male or Female unknown, along with a burial date.

There are no frills here. You won't find trees where John or Jane Doe decompose. You'll find no flowers, gravestones, or crosses. You could drive right by this fenced in plot of barren land sprinkled in gravel

149

and dust, clueless as to its purpose. You might easily mistake it for twenty acres of parking lot.

The women shuffle off the bus under the watchful eye of ItsHella County Sheriff's Deputies. The criminal pallbearers have arrived ready to mourn for the newly dead. But we don't mourn. We shed no tears. We are here to work and are glad to be away from the jail.

We don't dig the holes. They are dung out by a backhoe operator. He is usually nowhere to be found by the time we arrive. By counting the number of perforations that are in a row, we know how many bodies we will be depositing.

Waiting graveside is the volunteer Chaplain and Sister Mary Margaret. The Sister is always here dressed in her nun-wear, habit and all. She isn't like the nuns I remember in catholic school, all somber and angry. Sister Mary Margaret is very nice. She's also very old. When I talk to her, I always feel compelled to take her by the twiggish arm in support of her sparrow-like frame. When doing so, I'm rewarded with a smile that always reminds me of a withered apple.

When the first hearse arrives, six of us slide the casket out of the back of the vehicle and carry it to the first open grave. We stop at times to figure out the logistics of not tripping over our leg-irons. No worries, we only dropped a casket once. This brought on a wave of hysterical laughter. Embarrassment and awkwardness prompted the outburst. We didn't mean any disrespect.

This casket held the remains of Justin Anyone, his name written in black marker at the top of the particleboard casket that's covered in blue felt.

We carefully navigate around the hole and place Justin squarely on a casket lowing device stand that's positioned above the hole. Without mourners, there are no eulogies. The chaplain recited the 23rd Psalm and says some prayers for the dead. There have been times where family members were in attendance but more often not.

Sister Mary Margret blesses the casket with holy water shaken from a plastic bottle. Several inmates grabbed a fistful of dirt from a small mound of loosened earth and toss it on to the casket. Because I'm not sure why this is done, I don't partake. That box is going to see plenty of dirt soon enough.

One of the girls take holds of the manual crank and on cue begins to lower the casket. On its descent, we all sing "Amazing Grace." We are interrupted every few minutes as squads of fighter jets from the nearby Air Force Base whiz overhead.

When we're done here, we slide the lowing device stand over to the next empty grave and wait for the next coffin coach to arrive. Today we will do this six more times.

SEVENTEEN

—

The chain gang officers ignored my plea for a second chain gang trustee. Although they agreed that Maria would be the perfect candidate, the answer was still no. I was sure if I wore them down, they would give in. When Maria graduated from the chain, she got a job in the kitchen.

"It isn't so bad," Maria said. "I like it okay. It will help to make time pass quickly. I've been racking my brain about how I can generate some revenue in this place.

"Never fear my, Enterprising Sister," I said, "I have a stupendous new money making idea that can't miss."

Maria rolled the eyes.

I ignored that.

"According to my calculations you and I'll be rolling in the dough faster than you can say 'what if we get caught?'

"Really?"

"For reals," I said with spacious optimism. "I'm willing to bring you in on the ground floor.

Now Maria dishes out the cynical smirk.

"Your doubt hurts my feelings, Maria."

Maria sighed with disinterested eyes.

"Let's be reasonable here." I whine. "I mean really! Am I to blame for reality that often intercedes and thus mucks-up my plans? I'll admit to the occasional half-baked scheme, but that was six months ago, I was young."

"I refuse to get involved with anything that has to do with mice, dead pigeons or dancing bears." Maria said.

"No dancing bears?" I asked. "Oh well then..." I shrug the shoulders then turned and walk away.

Maria grabbed my arm and gave it a jerk.

"Cut the crap."

I faced her once more only this time I'm laughing like a hyena.

"Okay, okay." I look around the yard for a spot where we could have some privacy.

"Let's go over there and sit out of earshot.

We sat down on the gravel resting our backs on the chain link fence our legs jetting out in front of us.

"Here's the deal. When leaving the compound via the chain gang bus, I couldn't help but notice that the female side of tent city butts up against the visitor's public parking lot to the North.

"Yeah, so?"

"The sight of it brought to mind a spud-gun."

"What's a spud-gun?"

"A spud-gun is a pipe based cannon which uses air pressure to launch projectiles at very high speeds. They are built to fire chunks of potato, as a hobby, or to fire other projectiles. I'm thinking more on the lines of cigarette packages.

"You really think you can get cigarettes over that thorny fence?"

"I know we can. Launching a pack of smokes over the fence is but the work of an instant. Surely with your quick intelligence you can see that there is a gob of money in the thing."

Maria's pessimism began to wane.

"Have you worked out the details?"

I continued to pitch my plot strong.

"A field test is being conducted as we speak. Sharpshooter, a trusted friend and conspirator, is currently testing for distance, speed, explosive force, and that pesky noise factor."

Maria leaned in with interest her lips part slightly. I look at her mouth. It's beautiful. I force myself to look away. I'm talking to my shoes now.

"We need only get the cigarette package over the fence and dropped into the security camera's blind spot."

"And you think this is possible."

"Piece of cake," I said meeting her quizzical eyes.

"According to my calculations, we should be able to launch from a vehicle parked at the curb just across the street. The launcher can be shot out of a vehicle's sunroof or while laying on one's back in the bed of a pickup. Assuming everything checks out, the first delivery is scheduled Wednesday."

"So soon," Maria asked wide-eyed.

I answered by way of spacious grin.

The gravel was making my butt numb. I stood up.

"You feel like walking?"

"Sure."

I offer a hand and help Maria up.

"We will make the drop just before guards shift change and sun rise. I'm thinking around five-thirty. I can see a flurry of Ben Franklin's lining my books as we speak." I said.

I saw the dollar signs form in Maria's eyes.

One completely crumple-free filtered cigarette is a rarity and in extreme high demand. One smoke can be sold for two to five items. With twenty to a pack, it offers many lovely returns.

"I suppose you're interested in the financial aspect of this venture?"

"It appears we could clean up nicely." Maria said now smiling.

"Yes." I said with a toothy grin. "The recipient stands to make forty dollars per pack, minimally. We charge twenty-five at hand off. In the early stages, we will make a single pack delivery three times per week. If things go well we will double up on the deliveries.

All we have to do is take the fresh delivery to one of the Heads.

"The idea is ingenious." Maria said. "How is the twenty-five dollars distributed?

"The twenty-five gets split three ways. You and I get five dollars a pack. Sharpshooter receives fifteen.

"What do you want me to do?"

Your job, should you choose to accept it, will be to pick up the newly airborne delivery and hand it over to the person next in line to receive it."

"Will you cover me?"

"Of course I will."

"Why didn't you ask your obnoxious girlfriend Gabriella to do this?"

"Gabriella lacks a sense of diplomacy that you have a surplus of. You're a superior cultural attaché. You're an arbiter of goodwill, a natural go-between for this multicultural enterprise."

"That's nice of you to say."

"It's true. Besides, no one can stand Gabriella. They simply won't work with her. She may be dazzling and impressive, but I'm afraid this is the thing that has done her in."

"More rude and abrasive, but I get your point."

"It isn't her fault. Beautiful women, when not asleep, tend to be difficult. I openly admit that I too am more impressive asleep than awake."

"You got that right."

I narrow the eyes and grin.

"I'm talking about those women who are natural beauties. The kind most women hate at first sight. Women who are too pretty to be good. Being in the company of these women is frequently the equivalent of work."

"You're talking about my mother." Maria said staring into space reflectively.

"Than you understand. It is the inherent curse upon many women of impeccable loveliness. Their good looks get them everywhere blurring their perception of how most poor slobs live. It is as if fates main objective is to mollycoddle them. The unwarranted attention which they receive fogs the brain making it difficult for them to grasp the value of commending one's soul to God."

"That's so true." Maria said.

"Dating an attractive woman isn't for the faint of heart. Eventually, one grows tired of beautiful useless women, however well dressed. It may be more advantageous for one to seek out a homely woman with a squint and a good nature. If I had an ounce of sense I'd set my sights on an unpretentious, uncomplicated lump of clay that can be molded into something worthwhile."

"Interesting choice of words," Maria said.

"You know, Maria, it is only for the grace of enormous good fortune that you, with your devastatingly good looks, aren't stricken with the aforementioned malady."

"When you're right, you're right." Maria said grinning in spite of herself. "You aren't as dense about women as you let on."

"Perhaps not," I consider. "I possess a treasure trove of wisdom I've gleaned from all the women who have dumped me. But enough about my ongoing disappointments, what're your thoughts on the cigarette caper?"

As we walked, Maria pensively considered the plan that I had laid out before her. A pleased grin lit her pretty face and a squeal of excitement escaped her lips. She wore the expression of amusement, of joy, of beatific happiness. A look in short, of a woman who sees her way clear to laying her mitts on a considerable sum of hard cash. I too felt a giddy drunkenness of hope. There is something profound about the impending payday. It exercises a quickening effect on the human spirit.

"So," I said. "I suppose this means you're in?"

The operation went off without a hitch. Cancer packets sailed over the barbed wire fence right at zero five-thirty hours. They dropped smack dab into the designated safe zone. The procedure was a thing of beauty. At the end of the first month, deliveries were increased to two packets three times per week. The girls in the yard were smoking and joking, feeling chipper than whatnot. All was right with the world.

Upon retrieval, Maria placed the product underground to be dug up and distributed after chow. By underground, I mean just that. Hiding contraband inside the tents is a bad idea. Tents are tossed routinely. It is better to dig a hole where there is little to no foot traffic. A narrow path between the tents and the chain link fence is a good location.

It was one month into our lovely little monopoly when dark clouds appeared.

"We've got a problem." Maria announced upon returning from an early morning pick up. "The assistant head of kinfolk saw me make the pickup. She just mysteriously appeared. She wore a grin ear to ear, giving me a look that seemed to say 'got cha!'"

156

"Kinfolk didn't like our cutting them off from deliveries." I said. "They have got something up their sleeve."

"I think you're probably right," Maria said.

"Let's lay low for now. We'll get the skinny soon enough."

This news didn't come as a complete surprise. The Kinfolk rep on the outs was not conferring with our sharpshooter. There was no money transfer on their part. They had received three deliveries, but as of yet made no payment.

It was agreed upon up front that any monetary discrepancies would come out of my cut to be paid to the sharpshooter. This delinquent payment put me upside down to the tune of forty-five bucks.

The problem was that the Kinfolk had experience a recent 'changing of the guard', so to speak. The previous Head had been released. Any money made from the sale of cigarettes she took with her. The newly crowned queen, Ebony, was now liable for the balance due. She had been blindsided. She hadn't a clue what she was signing up for. She had no outside contacts. She was also unaware that this was a prerequisite to her new position.

Ebony had caught up with me a couple days ago in the dayroom.

"Look, Janie, if we can start with a clean slate, I'll guarantee on-time payment for the next delivery."

"I understand the position that you find yourself in, Ebony. The only clean slate I'll acknowledge is a zero balance."

"You pay five bucks for a pack of cigarettes and you expect me to give you twenty-five?"

Her face was the portrait of one who has been sold a bill of goods.

"The initial terms agreed upon were beneficial to all involved."

"Okay, okay. Look, I'm new at all this. Can you just throw me a bone here? I'm going to level with you. The girls want their menthols. If you could just keep them coming until I figure something out, I promise you'll be paid in full. You have my word."

I stood stoic and said nothing. I felt bad for her. I know she was under enormous pressure. I willed myself not to speak knowing that if I did, I'd cave.

"Please, you'd be doing me a huge favor."

"I'm sorry."

With a sympathetic smile, I turned and walked away.

"You're gonna be sorry," was the last thing I heard Ebony say.

+++

I was enjoying a walk around the compound. The evening was pleasant, the air slightly cools, and above was a clear sky lit with sparkly stars. The energy of the camp was buoyant. I wasn't the only one who enjoyed a little after dinner exercise. I nodded cordially to other strollers who returned the gesture. I felt at peace.

From behind me, I heard a heavy set of footprints clumsily navigating the gravel.

"Hey, Two-Ply, wait up," says a voice in dire need of oxygen.

I turned to see Ebony clumsily making her way toward me. The name-calling was my clue that the polite façade I've been privy to was over.

Ebony is a big girl whose body wasn't accustomed to the rigors of a brisk stroll. She broke into a less then elegant trot to catch up. When she reached me, I could tell by her labored breathing that she was no friend to her body. Everything about her said, 'why walk?' She's a monument to inactivity. This woman held that exercise was as unnecessary for anyone as it was uncomfortable for her.

"You know, Casper," Ebony said puffing and wheezing. "My people have been keeping a real close eye on you and that wetback friend of yours."

I shudder. I eye her with revulsion. I resisted the urge to grab a hand full of her hair and give it a good pull.

The blind anger I felt toward her, as she stood there smirking, was tempered by the pragmatic awareness that I must keep things agreeable.

"What're you, Cracker, a Pollock or something?" Ebony asked looking quizzically as if it were an important thing to know.

"I'm half American, half disgusted." I reply and take in a great gulp of air. "Let's walk shall we? By the way, her name is Maria." I said in a voice directly out of the Frigidaire. "You should endeavor to be half the woman she is."

I relaxed my pace to accommodate her bulk. Like a root canal, this bigot was something to be endured. Sometimes we have to just shut it and choke down our fair share of humble cow pie. I needed to put up with her crap long enough to find out what she was up to.

"Oh, I'm sorry." Ebony said in a tone void of sincerity. "Are you sweet on that beaner whore? She's a prostitute isn't she?"

It was as if she was grinding a pudgy chocolate finger right into a festering open wound. One more derogatory slur directed at Maria and I'm going to have to kill this woman. I could feel my blood begin to percolate. I pursed the lips and fought the surge of temper.

"Those whores are nasty bitches, don't you think?"

I stop walking. I can feel myself getting very angry.

Ebony stopped.

I pivot to face her. I watch as Ebony paused to wheeze and catch her breath. I hope she drops dead.

This bitch made good manners impossible. I glared at her. I have never hated a face more than I hated her face right now.

"That Cholo is a two-bit whore isn't she?" Ebony said with a sarcastic eyelift and cock of her head. She paused looking at me with great interest. She was waiting for me to detonate.

Something inside me snapped. A deep inhalation, a feeble attempt to calm myself, seemed only to make me see things more clearly. The lines on my face bunched up in hatred, my lips drew back from my teeth, and suddenly I scream, "You can go straight to Hell!" My voice was trembling with output in decibels greater than I had intended.

Ebony's grin expanded like a jack-o'-lanterns. A self-satisfied expression stung like a sledgehammer to the groin. The weight of this upset my sensibility and spurred me to one of those grand gestures, which now seem worth what they cost. With a bunched up fist, I swing. Before my knuckles met face, a hand reached in and caught my arm.

"Whoa there, let's take a couple steps back." Maria said.

She stepped in front of me, moving forward two paces. I involuntarily move back two.

"She's a vile piece of work." I murmur with clenched teeth.

I can feel my face flushed, the veins in my neck are bulging, and my eyes are screaming bloody murder. I've been this mad only one time before and I knew if I say another word, I'm going to start crying.

"Yes, Maria said. Her voice was calm and rational. "She's an ass, but we don't want to start a race riot."

Camilla stepped up beside Maria. The Beast was closing in fast.

"Are you okay?" Camilla asked with a careworn look.

I closed my eyes and lowered the head, my anger giving way to embarrassment. I was mortified that I lost my temper, but then I suppose somebody has to set a bad example.

I took a deep breath, forced a smile, and said, "I'm fine." Their presence calmed me.

"Two-Ply can take care of herself," Ebony piped up stepping closer. "Why don't you three scoot? If I need my tent cleaned, I'll give you girls a call."

The Beast, getting Ebony's meaning well, became red faced and tight jawed. I've seen this look before. Not a thing you want to be on the wrong end of. The Beast stepped forward intent on dealing a deadly blow. I take a step back in case she needs more room.

Camilla raised a restrictive hand. She looked at Ebony with a remarkable tolerance. Camilla's equanimity did impress me. However, I was really hoping that the Beast could work some of her magic here.

The Beast fumed glaring down at her feet, both fists in a tight ball. She grumbled something indiscernible that sounded like Spanish curse words.

Turning to me Camilla said, "We will be nearby."

I nod in appreciation.

"Thank you, I'll be fine now."

All three women turned and walked away.

I faced Ebony and said, "If your intention was to offend me, you have succeeded. Congratulations. I assume you have an actual point. I'd thank you to make it."

"It's like this, Casper. No one could figure out how you were getting all that nicotine into the yard. We've been watching you and Consuelo over there. Lo and behold, we discover that the Good Lord has been dropping nicotine sticks from the heavens practically right into your honkey hands every morning at 5:30. It'd be too bad if the cops got wind of these divine deliveries."

"Yes," I agree glaring down at the gravel. "That would be too bad."

"If you resume deliveries and toss in a couple extra packs as a goodwill gesture, I think we can keep our mouths shut."

"I'll take your threat under advisement."

I turned and walk. I walked in agitation, hard, and fast. I started to cry. I hate to cry over stupid stuff but this can't always be helped. Every time I have a good idea, the universe lifts its leg on it. It is disheartening.

I always feel better after a good cry. The sobbing that makes you shudder with convulsions are the best. This one was a light shower. It was already working its magic. I'm done trying to keep weakness and furtive tears to a minimum. Screw it. Right there in Psalms it says, "They that sow in tears shall reap in joy." There is no shame in doing a little sowing. Tears bear witness that a human being has the utmost courage, the courage to suffer. Sometimes things need to be wept out of our delicate systems.

In the course of my invigorating walk, I received from the cosmos -- God help me -- a fresh new big idea. It was a cigarette delivery scheme that was less risky, more streamline. This idea will catapult me out of the red for sure. The thrill of certain success surged through me. I gave a jump and high-fived the open air triumphantly. Things are beginning to look up. A providential change of fortune was on the horizon.

The laborious walk left me with a glow of rejuvenation. I was conscious of a clearer color in my cheeks and a fresh elasticity in my muscles. The future seemed full of promise. All my apprehensions were out of sight and I was sailing on the buoyant stream of my sunny disposition.

I was feeling lucky. I popped into the laundry tent to seek out a card game. Five white girls, my peeps, were huddled around a bottom bunk.

"Hey now," I say, "got room for one more."

The girls looked up. Janet grins and slides over to make room. She pats the cement floor revealing a swastika tattoo on her forearm.

"Sit, you can come in on the next deal."

I sit and grin.

"I should warn you. I'm feeling lucky."

"That's funny," Janet said. "When you sit down to play everyone at the table gets lucky."

"Screw you." I give her the elbow and narrow the eyes in a friendly way.

I broke even in cards.

After the game, I met with Maria and Camilla. I told them what Ebony said. We agreed that operation shutdown was inevitable. I choose not to spring the new idea on them just yet. This I'd do when all my eggs were in a tidy line.

EIGHTEEN

It is five a.m. in tent city. Maria and I are the only early risers. I finally managed to convince the chain gang officers that the trustee duties were too much for one person to handle. They agreed to allow Maria and me to work together. As there are only two of us on this work detail, we share a tent with twenty kitchen workers. At 0600 hours, the chain gang officers arrive to take us to "C" pod where the chain gang ladies lodge.

While the officers inspect and harangue the troops, Maria and I lay out three separate chains. Each measure approximately twelve feet in length. These chains will be attached to an ankle secured by a master lock. There are five women to a chain. We also gather a set of stripes for each member to be issued upon their return from the field.

The women exit the pod in single file. They fall into line by the chain where they wait to be shackled. They are wearing the customary stripes with spit shined black combat boots. Around each waist is an olive drab green military style tool belt. From the tool belt hangs a military canteen in a canvas carrier.

All seem on edge careful not to make one false move. Maria and I manacle each ankle while the officer's insult and further terrorize the already frightened fawns.

"Wilson," Officer Ahole bellows. "Why are your stripes wrinkled? Did you sleep in them? You look like shit."

Wilson shrinks. "No, Officer."

Officer Ahole steps in front of each girl. She eyes them with sour condescension.

"Speaking of shit, Gonzalez, is that what you used to shine your boots?"

"No, Ma'am," squeaked Gonzalez.

163

"You can write a five-hundred word essay on 'why my boots look like shit'."

"Yes, Ma'am."

"You losers have got to take some pride in your appearance. It is bad enough you can't march worth a shit. Your marching is an embarrassment. This is a problem that better be rectified or heads will roll. Do you birdbrains understand?"

"Yes, Officer." The group sounds off in unison.

The women march in military fashion out of the pod and down the halls. Maria and I walk along side helping the new girls to stay in step. The sound of the chain dragging on the floor makes it easy to identify the ones who insist on marching to their own beat.

This group is required to practice their marching every night. When the chain gang looks bad, the chain gang officers look bad and this makes them more unpleasant than usual.

A military cadence, a traditional call-and-response work song, is sung while marching. There are ten cadence calls adapted exclusively for the women's chain gang. These are required to be committed to memory.

While the ladies march out to the bus, Maria and I race to the kitchen to secure twenty lame-o bags and a ten gallon Igloo container of ice water. We place these items in the back of the bus and take our seats up front. An officer then drives the loaded bus to the portion of the compound where they keep the "Sheriffs Chain Gang Working" signs and a portable potty on wheels.

Maria hooks up the trailer full of signs to the Sheriff's department SUV that follows the bus. I grab the port-a-potty trailer and hook it to the hitch on the back of the bus. We never know where we're headed until we get there.

Once on location, the girls remain in the bus. The officer's in charge, there are two, go to each woman in turn and quiz them on one or all of the chain gang rules.

The rules are cumbersome, stupid statements. Here's an example: 'I am committed to perform my duties as a chain gang member with diligence, pride and Esprit de corps. I'll serve as an example of what

164

hard work and industrious efforts will produce.' Multiply this tedious twaddle by ten and it is easy to see how quiz time can be a alarming ordeal. It is a painful thing to eyewitness.

In reciting these rules, the omission of one word or syllable is grounds for public mortification and a writing assignment. Writing assignments are due at 0600 hours the following day. Few escape chain gang duty without some form of disfigurement to the writing hand or at the least a fat dose of carpal tunnel.

During the quiz and further humiliation segment, Maria and I place the "Sherriff's Chain Gang Working" signs in accordance with Department of Public Safety guidelines, or what seems right. There are five large triangular orange signs each to be seated in a metal stand. When we return to the bus and quiz time is over, we toss each girl a lame-o bag. When we're finished, eating it is time to pick up trash.

Once we're herded out of the bus, we all head to the rear of the vehicle. Maria hands out green hefty bags and fills canteens full of water.

With a scrub brush and cleaner in hand, I work my magic in the port-a-potty. When all is spic and span, I hand out shovels and rakes. It's time to pick up trash. As full bags accumulate, Maria and I will toss them into the trailer.

Grabbing an empty trash bag from the box, I motioned to Maria to follow. I gave her the bag to hold open while I pick up a handful of air and toss it into the bag. The guards don't hover. They stand back watching and chatting with rifles slung over their shoulders.

Maria and I were working about one hundred yards from the road. I was facing Maria; my back was to the traffic. She had a view of oncoming vehicles.

"Hey, Do you see that white Chevy Pickup that's coming our way?" Maria looked past me and grinned.

"It is a woman driver," Maria observed. "She's waving. Do you know her?"

"That's our Sharpshooter."

Maria shot me a look.

"What's she doing here?"

I grin and pretend to pick up something off the ground.

Maria opens the bag and I throw nothing in.

"It is my new big idea. I wanted to surprise you."

"Uh-oh, do I need to be concerned?"

"Don't be ridiculous. We're back in business, Maria. Sharpshooter is making a delivery. A pack of smokes and some ink pens."

You can't get pens in tent city, just crappy half pencils. Pens sell for three to five items. They move fast.

"I told Sharpshooter that we leave the compound around 0630 hours. She followed us here.

Picking up a couple stones, I throw them in the bag.

"Take it easy on the rocks."

"Right, sorry."

"Sharpshooter is making the drop at the last traffic barricade we put up. I made sure to put it around the corner, way out of sight."

Maria thoughtfully considered what I had said. She grinned.

"Have you thought out how you'll get this stuff back to the tents?"

"I have."

Every inmate returning from any work detail is strip searched before they are released to the tents. Despite this fact, contraband rolls into tent city with all the predictability of a scheduled train. If it's in a workstation and an inmate wants it, they take it. Items routinely snuck in include: Kool-Aid, tea bags for smoking and comfort foods galore. Because the officers don't seem to know what or how much of anything they should have on stock, nothing seems amiss.

There are no pockets in the striped pants, so items are placed in the waistband covered by the shirt, or tucked into a sock. Strip searches pose no threat to the felonious carrier due to the way they are conducted.

When returning to the tents from any work detail, inmates are brought to the dayroom. We are immediately placed in a holding cell. An officer takes six women at a time and directs them to the latrine where each inmate takes an open-air stall. A three-foot high concrete partition flanking left and right separate the toilets. There are no doors in here. The officer remains outside of the latrine while the girls disrobe.

All contraband is either placed in the trashcan or under a pile of clothing just removed. When everyone is naked, the officer enters. One at a time, each inmate is directed to lift the arms, turn, bend, spread and cough. When you're done, you're permitted to dress and the officer moves to the next person. In eight months, I've never seen an officer check the discarded clothing or waste bins.

Trash pickup lasts about one hour. Maria finishes throwing the last trash bags in the trailer and begins to gather the shovels and rakes. I jump into the back seat of the SUV and the officer swings around to each working sign. I jump out and toss the sign and stand into the front part of the trailer. I jump back into the back seat. The officer pulls up to the next sign. She never leaves the truck.

At the last marker, I find the prize. I take the package and quickly tuck it into my sock then grab the sign and stand.

I reenter the SUV. I adjust the package in my sock to ensure it is secure. Back at the bus, half the women are lined up to use the Port-a-potty. The other half are sitting on the ground chatting. When all are done with the restroom, they will fall into formation.

While in formation the women stand at attention. Leisure time is over. Ahole called the group to order.

"Listen up, Losers. We have a problem. If you think you're the problem step forward now, or things are gonna get bloody."

"What now?" was the expression that settled on the face of each startled, rigid soldier?

I scanned the ranks in an attempt to identify the culprit.

They all looked guilty of something.

In all likelihood, half of them were smuggling. During trash pickup, the girls routinely pocket cigarette ends. With some luck one could pick up enough tobacco for a decent sized rollie. Even if you don't smoke, it serves as excellent barter.

The officer eyed the girls with a great deal of displeasure. She walks up and down the line giving each woman the critical head to toe with a sneer. The other officer isn't so bad, but this one is an uber sadistic bitch. A woman created in our worst nightmare, she is incapable of mercy or pity.

Ahole is a sawed-off runt of a woman, unattractive and as wide as she's short. She was certainly no credit to the man's polyester uniform she wore. It looked as if she had been poured into it and forgot to say 'WHEN!'

Her aura is a fetid and murky blur of festering hatred. Her specialty is to antagonize while wearing a smirk of disdain. The embodiment of hostility, this wench is mean for sport. Her mere presence could scare the life out of a corpse.

Officer Ahole throws her whole toxic self, heartless and soulless, into her work. She's a monster who loves to use the misfortune of others as an ointment for her shortcomings.

We all know some of the worst natural catastrophes of the Twenty-first century: Hurricane Katrina, Haiti earthquake, "Coming Soon" -- the Battle of Armageddon, and the most devastating by far: Cellulite.

Deputy Ahole had a serious condition of hips, ass, and no tits. Hers is a posterior that struck fear into the hearts and minds of every chair. She's a woman in her late-thirties who's acutely aware that with age comes sagging, dimpling, unsightly skin, a sluggish metabolism, and the guarantee of a fatter, uglier, angrier her with thicker ankles. This is a frightening reality. We all must pay.

"Sanchez, Doughy," bellowed Officer Ahole.

She performed an about-face and was staring directly at Maria and me.

 "Someone has cigarettes on their person. Do you know who that might be?.

I felt the effects of a purely physical anxiety. I think I'm going to be sick. The cigarette package pressing against my ankle felt like a hot branding iron. I could feel my face turn a lighter shade of pale. Things have taken a very ugly turn for the worse.

"No, Ma'am." We responded in unison.

Officer Ahole swung back around and faced the group.

I was staring at the officers back, my face like a doe caught in headlights.

Maria grabbed my wrist and pulled my arm down to my side. I must've been biting my closed fist.

Maria leaned in and whispered, "Try to act normal."

"Yes, of course."

The trouble is I've never really known what normal looked like.

"We know who you are." Ahole announced to the group.

Here it comes. I expect her to whip around any second now. I inhaled deeply in an attempt to calm myself. It didn't help. I wanted to run, but knew that was a bad idea. Crying might seem suspicious.

"We planted that pack of cigarettes in this field as a test and you failed. Now the entire group will be penalized."

This statement brought on a mild sense of relief. I've seen them pull this trick before. But then she might be screwing with me.

"I'll say this one more time, I strongly advise you to step forward. If I need to drag your ass out of formation things are going to get bloody."

A very long second past before the nervous perpetrator stepped forward. The rest of us exhaled with visible relief.

The officer stepped to the wrongdoer and put out an opened palm. As the woman reached into her waistband for the goods, she began to cry.

"Oh my God," wailed Officer Ahole. She was addressing the other chain gang officer.

"Sissy-La-La here is crying. Can you believe this shit?"

In response, the other officer shook her head in the negative and offered a frown. This was more participation than she typically put forth which is why we all liked her. She was standing off to the side holding her rifle like it was a pogo stick. She was a big-boned, white woman, thirtyish and butcher than a pub full of lumberjacks. She has a managerial style that I've always admired. It hovers somewhere between "hands off" and "I don't want to get involved". Her nickname to this group was Do-little. Ahole had a nickname too, but it involves graphic language that's sure to offend.

"There is no crying in the chain gang," Officer Ahole said, screaming into the face of Sissy-La-La.

The sheepish woman placed the packet of cigarettes into the officers open palm. Her lips twisted downward in an exaggerated frown, tears were still flowing, and she was struggling to catch her breath.

"Get back into formation. You make me sick. I advise you to save some of those tears for later. When I get done with this group, they're gonna want to kill you. Then you'll really have something to cry about."

Sissy-La-La turned on her heels and fell back into formation. Poor thing looked pathetic. This experience is sure to leave hideous emotional scarring. I thanked God I wasn't her.

Naturally, Ahole wasn't done with her yet. "I don't know if you realize." She leans in conspiratorially. "You're surrounded by convicted felons. These girls don't get weepy over a little ol' murder, especially when someone has it coming.

"Doughy, Sanchez, front and center."

The threat of humiliation puts the chop-chop in our step.

"I want you two to collect everyone's canteen and fill it to the brim with water, NOW." Ahole slammed the butt of her rifle into the dirt. I half expected it to discharge.

"Yes, Ma'am," we replied and without delay started to collect canteens.

With all fifteen containers in tow, we headed for the back of the bus to top them off.

"That was a close one," I said. "I'm getting to old for this horseshit."

Maria uncaps a canteen and places it under the IGLOO cooler. She laughs.

"You should've seen your face, I was sure you were going to start crying. You're the Sissy-La-La."

"Oh sure yuck it up, everything is fun and games until the senior citizen keels over with a heart attack."

Maria gives me two full canteens.

"Okay, Grandma, I think you better stash those smokes in the back of the bus for now. I've got a feeling we may be in for some rigorous training. It is better to be safe than stupid."

Maria smirks as she topped off another canteen.

"You're probably right."

I reached into my sock and grabbed the precious cargo. I placed it into a bag of rags in the back of the bus.

"Sanchez, Doughy, let's get a move on," barked the human snapping turtle.

Maria loaded my arms with full canteens and rushed to finish the rest. The containers were cold and wet and felt good against my naked arms. I hurried back to the formation and offered a canteen to each woman. When all canteens were returned, it was time to get this party started.

The rigid soldiers are standing at attention, their eyes wide with unease.

"We're going to be marching up that hill."

Using her rifle as a pointer, Ahole motioned to a hill that looked like it might be easier to traverse using a rope and climbing harness.

"Dress right, DRESS," Ahole hollered in baritone.

This command requires individuals, except the one on the extreme left side, to raise their left arms parallel to the ground and turn their heads to the far right in order to get the proper distance from each other. This is maintained until the command, "Ready, FRONT." At which point, the individuals return to the position of attention.

"Ready, FRONT," barks the Ahole.

"Right, FACE."

"Take out your canteen. Place the canteen in your left hand. Hold it out in front of you with arm stretch out perpendicular to the ground. Do you retards know what perpendicular means?"

Maria and I looked at each other and rolled the eyes.

She meant parallel.

"You'll carry your canteen like that while you march, no bending your elbow. I repeat, do not bend the elbow. You bend your elbow you get a writing assignment."

"Sanchez, Doughy, march these nitwits up that hill.

Maria and I took our place to the left of the formation. Maria was close to the front. I brought up the rear.

171

We gave the order, "forward, MARCH and a left, left, left, right, left," to help the girls stay in step.

Midway up the hill elbows were bending and the girls were grumbling. Officer Ahole supervised from down below and ordered us to march in silence.

"Clemens, fifteen-hundred word essay on why I shouldn't bend my elbow."

"Jones, you too," The officer bellowed jovially. She's such a bitch.

No one escaped penalty. I would not want to be the woman who picked up those cigarettes.

When we returned to the bus the ladies were beat. The thought of writing all night dampened the spirits of all.

When we return to the compound, Maria and I toss the bags full of debris into dumpsters and remove the trailers for the bus and SUV.

Back in "C" pod, we issue a fresh set of stripes and under garments to the women. The atmosphere was as dreary as Schindler's List. We handed out fresh uniforms while all waited in line to be strip-searched. Maria and I were searched last.

"Get dressed, you have two seconds. I want to get the hell out of here."

Extracurricular activities had bitten into her free time and she was obviously annoyed by this. Maria and I dressed in a panicked rush. I grabbed from the shelf whatever was in front of me. I absently slide on a tent-sized pair of pink underwear. I put on a pink sports bra, stripes, and socks. I had stashed the smokes under a pile of stripes earlier and now tucked them securely into my sock.

"You two get the hell out here now!" barked Officer Ahole foaming at the mouth.

Maria was out the door. I was right behind her, when I realized I hadn't put on a pad. I have an incontinence problem. It's not too terrible, just some leakage when I run, laugh, cough, and sometimes when I breathe. I'm not even fifty and I'm already accumulating the unpardonable flaws of aging.

This is how it all begins: The graying hair, the tiny crows-feet around my eyes, and the deep lines from my nostril to the corner of my mouth which will soon extend down to my pointy chin, paving the way for a fresh set of jowls. This is tangible proof that death has begun to manifest itself in my body. Observing these telltale signs is like overhearing your demise waging a campaign. I think back on a time when my skin fit me exactly. What happened?

It was hot today and I drank a lot of water. I have to pee, but know it is pointless to ask to use the restroom. I grabbed a pad off the shelf, ripped it from its packaging, and shoved it between my legs.

It takes about five minutes to walk from "C" pod to the tents. We walked at a swift pace down the hallway.

The pad between my legs was moving about frantically in those big granny panties. These pads were not the thin, low profile type with adhesive. Oh no. These pads were principally designed to absorb buckets of blood and clots. They are often issued in hospitals for use after a hysterectomy or abortion. It is a product that's a testament to how fun it is to be a woman.

I tried to walk normal. But, it was necessary to keep my thighs close together, as if I were trying to hold a coin between my knees. My gait didn't feel natural. I knew in my heart that I looked suspicious.

Maria jerked my arm, like she does, and gave me a stern look. She probably thinks I've lost my grip on the contraband. She doesn't know about my bladder.

What could I do? We were walking too fast. The striped pants were exceptionally baggy. This didn't help matters either.

I found myself intermittently using my hand to push the pad back into position. This was risky business and as it turned out, rather pointless. Before long, the pad had worked its way out of the tent panties. It slid down my thigh and the next thing I know it was loitering about the knee.

Obviously, this pad had it in for me. Considering every angle I couldn't see how any good could come of this. This sanitary napkin had my full and undivided attention. So much so, that I hadn't noticed that old Officer Ahole was watching me.

"Doughy." She screeched, eyeing me with suspicion.

I look at Maria and sent her a telepathic message.

173

"It's been nice knowing you. I'm going to die now."

Maria seemed to understand. Her whole being radiated an sympathetic UH-OH.

Ahole pointed to an unoccupied supply closet to the right. "Get in there."

Oh boy. I braced myself for another unpleasant installment.

"Drop your pants and spread'em," ordered the annoying wench.

I turned and pulled down the pants and panties simultaneously. Those parachute panties, that were my foe only minutes ago, became my salvation as they draped over the paraphernalia in my sock.

Where the pad went, I couldn't tell you. By way of psychic hit, I had a vision of it lying idle in the center of the hallway.

I bent and spread the cheeks. She made her inspection. I had half a mind to ask her to pass me a cigarette. This thought made me laugh, but only on the inside.

"Okay, Straighten up," ordered Ahole.

I recovered from my vulnerable position and look squarely at my tormentor. I looked into the eyes that dotted her flabby face. I felt slapped. We were standing close together in the cramped quarters of the supply closet. My five foot something was looking down on her four foot nothing. So close, were we that if a heap of someone's steamy vomit were placed before my eyes, I couldn't have been more horrified or disgusted.

Just when you think you've already reached the summit of humiliation, the universe dishes out a spoonful more. I was too angry to control the hatred in my eyes. Her doughy well-fed face was the picture of uncertainty. I felt a sudden urge to punch those ten pounds of flesh right in the mouth. With an attitude of offense, I said nothing.

Unaffected by my scorn, Ahole blinked nonchalantly, opened the door and waddled into the hall.

I've never told anyone about my incontinence problem. It is too embarrassing. Sure, I told my Mom, but she's not just anyone. She told me to do kegel exercises down there. I said okay but I don't feel like it. To have explained the situation to this murky splotch, Ahole, would be inviting the possibility of some horrid nickname like pissy pants, a moniker that would soon earn common usage. Who needs all that?

Chain gang trustee was a great job, but every second subjected to her exploits made all things unpleasant. I can become used to all sorts of oppression, in time, but I feel I've met my match. Truth is I've had my fill of Officer Ahole. I need her crap like a moose needs a hat.

I could no longer suffer any more abuse from this super-fatted terrorist. I suppose I should thank her for making me more proficient at ignoring insult. I decided that I'll no longer be a witness to her poisoning the world with her malice.

When I returned to the yard, I put in a tank order requesting a job change. I handed the request to an officer who I knew would push it through for me. They aren't all soulless cretins. After turning in the tank order, I retired to my tent.

Maria was lying on her bunk, which was just below mine. She seemed to be enjoying a mystery novel. I pushed her legs aside to make room for me to sit.

"I've had it with that bitch." I bellyache.

"What are you talking about?" Maria asked closing her book and sitting up.

"That bleak spectacle Ahole that's who. I put in a tank order for a job reassignment." Leaning in conspiratorially I asked, "Can you take over delivery pickup?"

"I'd love to." Maria said with a grin. "What happened?"

"I can't say. I'm simply too old for this crapolla. I'm done. That barge of blubber needs to be brought down a couple pegs. She's out of control."

"Too true," Maria said. "Her day will come. Are you sure you can't hang on a little while longer?"

I narrowed the eyes. "What're you up to now?"

"I'm afraid I can't say," Maria said with a grin.

I was reassigned to another workstation rather quickly. I'll give you the details later. I was playing a game of cards in the laundry tent when I noticed a group of girls crowded around. One of the girls had received a kite from her friend who was a current chain gang member. I excused myself from the game. As she began to read the kite aloud, I saunter over to join the listeners.

This morning the universe sought glorious retribution in the form of a drive-by. A deserving deputy Ahole was hit squarely in the posterior with a paint ball in the shade of a patriotic pink. We all basked joyfully in her horror and mortification. It was a thing of beauty. Heartfelt thanks go out to all responsible.
Signed with sincere gratitude,
All Chain gang members: past, present, and future.

I joined the girls in a hoot and holler fest. This prank has Maria written all over it. I found her sitting at a table in the dayroom. She was working her way through a crossword puzzle.

I sat across from her. Wearing my chimpanzee grin I said, "Pink was a nice touch."

Looking up from the word game, she returned the grin with one even wider.

"It was, wasn't it?"

"Once again, Maria, I find myself thunderstruck by your brazen ingenuity. With one fell, judicious swoop you have managed to bring joyful hope into the hearts and souls of the troops. Our Matron Saint of lost causes, you're forever on a mission of mercy performing hideous acts of retaliation against the all too deserving."

"Just a little rule-bending in service of a greater good." Maria explained. "Sometimes, in the fulfillment of our happiness, somebody has to get hurt".

I looked at her with wide-eyed fascination taking her in through the pores. Now this is a proclamation worthy of some reflection. If this is not written in the big book of important sayings, it should be submitted.

"I couldn't have put it better myself."

I shower her with a look of admiration.

176

"I am one of many who cannot thank you enough for this random act of terrorism. The voices of one hundred Angels could not express our gratitude."

Once again Maria has proven herself to be above criticism and impossible not to love.

NINETEEN

There is something very quaint about tent city in the evening hours. After a long day at work, the girls like to smoke, joke, and hunker down into their beddies. It is much like a comfy cozy slumber party, all lighthearted and pleasant.

It was a perfect night to be in bed with a good book listening to the tic, tic of raindrops bouncing off a sturdy tile roof. It was a lousy night to be housed in Sheriff Porcupino's tent city, where the tent tops have the effective water repellency of Bounty -- the quicker picker upper.

Occupying a top bunk offers several disadvantages. Becoming an umbrella for the lower bunk is just one of them. August is monsoon season in the Valley of the Blistering Sun. At the first sign of high winds and unending cloud cover, one is wise to secure as many plastic can liners as can be smuggled out of the dayroom.

The key is to get from your tent to the dayroom before cloud burst. This is precisely where I fell short. In my naiveté, I hadn't realized that the tent seams not only held the tent together, but also served as a water inlet providing complete saturation of the contents therein. Foul weather conditions provide a legitimate reason for us to agonize over our merciless living conditions. This is not to say that tent city doesn't have its good qualities. I'm sure it looks great from outer space.

I was hopeful that I might finish a couple chapters of a Janet Evanovich paperback, but I dozed off. When I came to, the book I was holding looked a lot like oatmeal and I was soaking wet. In a panic, I leapt off my soggy crib top and brave my way into the storm.

A nice steady soaker chased everyone off the yard. My first step out of the tent found my prison issued pink sock and canvas shoe submerged in puddle to just above the ankle. The other involuntarily followed. Crap!

178

The rain was brutal and relentless. It had taken to swirling sheets with the wind catching me in gusts, soaking my stripes, and plastering my hair to my face. By the time I got to the dayroom, I was drenched, shivering, and in a wretched mood.

I sloshed my way to the trustees supply closet. I was too annoyed to be concerned with the fact that I had no authority to be in there. I snagged a handful of suicide bags and made my exit. I responded to the on-duty trustee's disapproving remarks by waving a carefully selected finger in her face. I wasn't in the mood.

I returned to my tent soaked to the bone. It was oddly liberating to know that I couldn't get any wetter. I tore the plastic bags and draped them across the metal tent framing just above my bunk. Fellow top bunkers looked on in awe. I placed additional bags on my already soaked bedding. I hoped that once I was underneath, my body temperature would bring the damp cocoon to a comfortable ninety-eight degrees. This might explain why my grades in physics put my GPA in the shitter (pardon the vernacular).

I slide into the wet bedding, in wet clothes, and felt my skin crawl.

"YUK! This is complete bullshit!" I cried my face crinkled in disgust.

"Complete bullshit is right," agreed a top-bunker to my left.

"This place is a shit hole," said another.

"We're all gonna be sick." said a congested voice.

Our whining woke a few of the bottom dwellers.

"Shut the hell up."

Feeling pissed off and misunderstood, one of the girls jumped down from her drenched bunk. She went over and punched that stupid blabbermouth right in the head.

Oh sweet, senseless act of brutality. Hit her again, I wanted to say. My better-self glowered at me.

I laid there for a few minutes telling myself it was just a matter of getting used to. I'm a firm believer in denial. I typically ignore most things with the tolerance of one who expects worse to come. When things stay the same, I count myself lucky. Sometimes, if you wait long enough things will just self-correct. Take for example, how my incarceration naturally cured my Starbucks addiction or say how death, being the great equalizer, can cure cancer.

Grossed out by my damp clammy flesh, I rolled off my bunk and went back into the dayroom. Although the rain had subsided, my mood remained partly cloudy.

In order to procure dry threads, I'll have to ask a guard. Clothing and blankets are stored in a locked linen closet located in the dayroom. To provide me waterless-wear would not be that much of a hassle. Not really. Nevertheless, I went in knowing that it would be easier to get permission from Smokey the Bear to start a forest fire.

It is generally known that any attempt to get an officers attention is looked upon as a grave imposition and commonly met with a frumpy, put-upon frown. Another disadvantage I had working against me was the time. It was after midnight. Guards working the swing shift may be walking upright, but in every practical sense, they are as dead as a beaver hat.

Upon entering the dayroom, I scanned the largely uninhabited space for an on-duty officer. I was in luck. There she was right out in the open. It was difficult not to notice that this officer bore a striking resemblance to something out of the movie "Night of the Living Dead". As graveyard officers go this one was marginally okay, but she had to be careful not to drag her knuckles when she walked. It was as if nature intended to make a gorilla then, last minute, changed its mind.

She was a woman of fifty-something with a grayish-brown aura suggestive of a bad diet, bad choices, and bad life. Prior dealings with her gave me reason for alarm. She was a spiteful official and took pleasure in being so. Her ineptitude was staggering. She wore the ravages of booze and discontent, which spoke of a past that was plentiful in horror and disappointment. She gave off the smell of stale cigarettes mixed with the scent of bourbon filtered through an overtaxed liver.

On my fifth, "Excuse me, Officer," she raised a crayoned eyebrow. There was, in her eye for a moment, the sense of a Raid Fogger looking meaningfully at a cockroach.

"WHAT!" She spewed with the leathery harsh voice of a longtime smoker. It was obvious she resented my very existence.

"Pardon me, Ma'am." I stammer wringing the hands with force to calm my nerves. "My clothes are soaked through as is my bedding. Is it possible to receive a dry issue, Ma'am?"

My question made her wince.

"Not possible," the officer rasped out, alto voiced, two drags short of lung cancer.

"But, but..."

I tried to expound but the look on her face stopped me cold.

Every digit of her blood pressure was showing right there on her weary face. Glaring at me, she leans in closer and with a tired, practiced contempt she said, "I'm beginning to lose my patience with you hoodlum!"

I felt the warmth of her bad breath on my face. My stomach curdled.

"With all due respect, Officer, if you had patience you would not lose it."

The officer's jaw dropped giving me a distasteful view of her brownish stained teeth. She breathed through her nose and I could hear what work every breath was for her. Both agitated and perplexed by the fact that I hadn't gone away yet, she ordered, "Shut your F*&% mouth and get back to your bunk!"

Well, I reflected. Doesn't this just solidify the social tone of this place? I should've known better than to attempt a rational conversation with this primate. She possesses one of those stereotypical minds that run along channels of stock responses and dismal possibilities. The thing I need most from her is her absence.

I've exceeded my daily allowance of insult for one evening. Try as I might, I never seem to get used to this sort of treatment. I have half a mind to write a tell-all letter to the Arizona Examiner. I mean to do just that if my stationary ever dries.

With a face as blank as enamel, the officer pushed me aside. She lumbered past like she was dragging an enormous ball and chain behind her. She was likely en route to meet with her best buddy -- Jack

Daniels. A life giving snort and liberation from the dreadful pain of reality was all she really needed.

I've come to expect such apathy and uselessness from the hired help around here. No worries. That which is impossible isn't a deterrent. The impossible doesn't bother me. If this problem couldn't possibly be resolved then obviously, it must be resolved impossibly.

What's important is that I harbor no ill will toward the officer. I will mention that she is rumored to have had sex with circus animals.

Moving from my temporary psychoses, I decided on a trip to the potty for a good think. A nice, solitary number-two often lifts my spirits. Upon exiting the latrine I spied two wall mounted hand dryers. I pointed the nozzles toward my wet pant legs and popped both oversized silver buttons with my palms. I enjoyed the warm sensation. While being blown, I noticed Officer Orangutan had called together the dayroom trustees. She ordered them to gather waste from bins for a trash run. When she and her minions file out of the dayroom, I sprung into action.

I headed to the now empty trustee station that consisted of a desk surrounded by four cheap white plastic scoop chairs. On three of the chairs were blankets placed strategically to serve as padding for rear ends that already had ample cushion. I was obligated to correct the overdo. Very pleased with myself, I hurried out the dayroom with blankees in hand.

The bags above my bunk were straining from the weight of tainted rainwater. Climbing up to my platform, I pushed up on the brownish yellow liquid allowing it to stream out of the plastic. The heavy runoff made a loud crashing sound as it went splashing to the cement slab below.

"What the Hell?" shrieked my dry and comfortably resting bunky below.

"I'm sorry!" I said with dripping sarcasm, "Have I disturbed your shuteye?" I wanted desperately to unleash a fire hydrant on her.

I stripped my wafer-thin mattress of all things wet and redressed it with the dry stiff scratchy OD green blankets. I removed my damp clothing, placed my near dry self inside the sandpaper coverlets, and pulled it snuggly over my head. I slept like I hadn't slept in a year.

TWENTY

A sour, defensive attitude and the unmistakable impression that you're dangerously close to snapping point is all one really needs to achieve a satisfying incarceration. One of the best ways to keep those pesky inmates within foul breath distance away is by feigning insanity. This is a bit tricky, as most of us have spent a lifetime trying to convince others that we're normal. Now when we need to "just be ourselves", we aren't sure what that looks like. No worries. I'm here to help.

An inkling of mental illness really freaks people out. This brings to mind an inmate by the name of Betty.

Betty is a white girl, short and stout. She must've been around nineteen years old. She had the look of a woman who would soon look just like her frumpy, bread baking, arts and crafts making, Mother. Some things are just a given.

I had suffered the great misfortune of meeting Betty while trapped in solitary confinement. I only had to put up with her for less than twenty-four hours, but it had been a segment of time that left an unsightly scar on my soul.

At first glance Betty appeared nontoxic and so initially, I played nice. This was my first mistake. Have you ever met a child who suffered from an extreme case of maternal depravation? Once they've learned that there is no point trying to get Mommies attention, they glom on piteously to whoever happens to pass by. If you're polite and show the slightest hint of interest, they will latch onto you with the vivacity of a rabid snapping turtle. This was Betty.

I didn't ask because I wasn't interested, but I'll bet that Betty was put in the hole for being a general, all-purpose pain in the ass.

As you know, I do my best to avoid human interaction. But then my better-self intercedes and tells me to stop being a douche. And so at first, I gave into Betty's request that I play cards and some other asinine game she had concocted. Being a little slow on the up-take, this

183

horseplay lasted a full half day. It wasn't until I found myself at the end of my rope and ready to hang from it when the penny finally dropped. I promptly turned into the ice queen or from Betty's point of view, Mommy.

I became in every way unavailable.

Betty began to sulk audibly. She mumbled hateful obscenities and threw personal items at the wall with all the high spirits of a mental patient.

I fill the ear-holes with the stuffing from a menstrual pad. I lay stock still in a fetal position, on my bunk, facing the dingy brick wall. I am a rock. I am an island. I will not be moved.

The med nurse stops by the cell just before chow. I hear Betty tell her that she's depressed and suicidal. She needs her meddies. The Med nurse will need to do a records check before she can willy-nilly hand out pillies. The next morning, the med nurse stops by and hands Betty, not one pill, but an entire sheet of God-knows-what.

What the hell? It really is none of my business, or not yet.

By noon, Betty has taken all the pills. The empty packet with what looked like twelve pills popped out, was on the floor in clear line of sight of my top bunk, no doubt, so that I might see what I had made her do.

Leaning over my bunk, I look down at Betty. Her arms are sprawled lifeless and limp, her stupid face is sheet-white, and her mouth is open wide.

Oh for God's sake, I don't need this.

"Betty," I holler, "Hey, Betty." She doesn't budge. I jump off the top bunk and give her a shake, still nothing. I gave her a punch in the arm then a few sharp head-slaps for good measure. She was still unresponsive. I was just about to pull her hair when my better-self intervened, barking out some maddening chastisement. Okay, okay.

I proceed to bang on my cell door until the guard in the bubble hears me. "What in the hell is your problem Doughy," barks my nemesis through the P.A. system. I hate that guard and she hates me more.

"Suicide attempt," I holler.

Within minutes, Betty is removed from my cell by stretcher.

As you can see, things turned out rather nicely.

What's my point? I'm getting to it.

So, the other day I'm walking around the tents, desecrating those pesky calories, when what to my wondering eyes should appear? It's Betty.

When you have been here as long as I have, you have the opportunity to see people come and go and come back again.

Betty was walking erratically, looking down at the gravel, while mumbling to herself like a madwoman. When she came through, I noticed that the masses parted like the Red Sea. Betty was acting crazy personified and was working this crowd like a flailing carp at the end of a fishing line. Her bazaar behavior was inspiring. I had obviously underestimated the girl. I can admit that.

The muttering was a nice touch, but she had outdone herself when she started holding a cardboard sign skyward as a distress signal to be seen by planes flying overhead.

True enough, we were very close to the International Airport and we did get a great deal of sky traffic. The sign she's holding up now reads: "NEED BEER".

The inmates titter at this while making greater the distance between them and her. They avoided her as if she had, tattooed to her forehead, the mark of the Beast. I was impressed.

I approach Betty as she puts down the inventive "NEED BEER" sign. She regards me with a sneer and picks up another sign.

This one reads: "BEEN KIDNAPPED. PLEASE HELP!"

"Hi, Betty, It is so good to see that you're not dead yet." I say with a wide grin and in a way that I hoped might thaw the icy chill.

She gave me a sour look and said, "What do you want?"

It was apparent that she didn't forgive me for making her attempt suicide. I had her figured for the kind who just won't let a thing go.

I cross my arms and arch my back to get a good look skyward. "Soooo, how is the whole sign thing working out for ya?"

Betty's arms were feeling the burn from holding them in an unnatural position for an extended period. She grimaces at the discomfort but soldiers on.

185

"To date and for the record, not even one commercial airline has acknowledged my S.O.S. petition." Betty said bitterly.

"Perhaps they can't see you."

"Ohhhh, they see me alright." She said, kicking the gravel savagely. "When I get out of this joint, you can bet your bottom dollar, I'm going Greyhound."

+++

As jobs go, I give KP duty an enthusiastic three thumbs up. Kitchen detail highlights include, unlimited snacking and ample amounts of screw-off time. A word of caution, weight gain is more the norm than unusual in jail. If you can't fit back into the street clothes that you came in with, you'll leave in a one-size-fits-all white paper jumpsuit. This has been a public service announcement.

Where KP duty is concerned, when all is said and done, more is said than done. If you have turned your life over to lethargy and possess as much natural laziness as a corpse then kitchen work is for you. The mission statement for this work environment should read: "Nothing's impossible for those who don't have to do anything".

The perks don't end here. In the kitchen wild life abounds. This isn't to be confused with the food served which has all the vital life force of a doorknob. No, I'm speaking more of a biodiversity that appeals to both the entomologist and nature lover alike.

The whole place is congested with living organisms. Mice, cockroaches and I swear I saw a monkey. I love all God's creatures big and small. Cockroaches typically stay out of sight, but are often discovered whilst we're moving pots and stackable trays to and fro. The Phoenician cockroach is about the size of a well-endowed male orangutans thumb. The sight of them often creep people out. I find it impossible not to admire their ability to withstand the crushing weight of a two-hundred pound shoed mammal and saunter away unscratched. Then too, their evolutionary advancement in winged flight is nothing less than phenomenal. I've always wanted to fly.

During the time that I was working in the kitchen the drainage system was clogged. Water and whatnot, had backed up through the drainage gratings in the kitchen floor. The smell was revolting. The problem remained for well over a month. When this sort of thing happens, all female kitchen personnel are required to wear men's size thirteen, black knee high rubber boots. This foot wear was a lovely complement to the requisite blue hair net. The standing water only came up to a couple inches above the ankle.

Before the end of our shift, we're required to cleanup. Water is a necessary evil at this juncture. We're urged not to use too much water, it aggravated the existing drainage problem. Sloshing about in these flooded conditions made walking without a fall a bit tricky. Falls are inescapable. These torrential circumstances made it necessary to walk in timid baby steps.

The Environmental Health Services Division of ItsHella County is responsible for ensuring that food handlers in the county comply with Environmental Health Codes. Government institutions, being above the law, need not concern themselves with said trifling inconveniences.

"Health, Smealth," say jail administrators. "Plumbers are an expense that might bite into our yearly 'cost-cutting' incentive bonus!"

Mice can be found throughout the encampment, but prefer to assemble in infinite masses around the kitchen. Mouse sighting account for the occasional high pitch screams which can be heard during any given KP work detail.

The mice here are as cute as buttons, but they can be annoying. The bolder ones can be found just inches from your tray while you're trying to eat. I don't like anything staring at me while I'm shoveling in the provisions. Nevertheless, there they sit, on their haunches, little paw hands in prayer position. They look up at you with a pitiful expression.

"Please feed me. I'm starving to death."

It gets to me every time.

The majority of women here aren't a-scared of a little old mouse. Due largely to our innate maternal instincts, these fuzzy little hamsters are well fed. People food is all they know. I wouldn't say this contributes to the infestation problem, but I wouldn't rule it out either.

A similar condition exists on the Women's side of tent city regarding pigeon infestation. This invasion doesn't exist on the Men's side of the fence.

This reminds me of a time, while sitting on my bunk in my assigned tent, when I noticed a wacked pair of polyester trousers slink in through the back gate, accompanied by several sets of patent leather shoes. The scene was as out of place here as a tampon machine in a retirement home. Correct me if I'm wrong, but didn't polyester slacks go out of fashion around the time of disco and big sideburns? Who can keep up? Anyway, next thing I know the women are in frenzy, ransacking their bunks in search of pencil and paper.

It turns out to be Sheriff Porcupino. The girls wanted his autograph.

"What the hell for?" I marvel. The group appeared divided. One half excited devotees, the other half cold, detached, and sickened by Porcupino's presence. You love the guy or you loathe him.

Old Joey was followed closely by his very own portable Paparazzi. He walked toward the swooning fan club members with a Master of the Universe swagger. Sherriff Porcupino is a handsome man. That's assuming that you find W.C. Fields attractive. The bulbous nose look is an acquired taste.

I remember the first time I met that nose in person. No question about it, it is totally out to get him. A veritable train wreck situated squarely in the center of his podgy face, it draws the on-comers' eyes to it like dust bunnies to a vacuum hose. Sure, you try your best to be well-mannered and not stare at the peculiar mound of flesh, but the harder you try not to look the more impossible it becomes. It isn't something I'd want for myself. If I had to confront that snout every time I looked into a mirror, I'd kill myself. Time, which is no friend to the ugly, has turned Sherriff Porcupino into a caricature.

If you're under the impression that Arizonans love the old porcupine, think again. His is a name that often excites a violent dislike. With time, his character becomes more and more repugnant without any corresponding sign that he gets it. Porcupino is repeatedly voted into Office by senile retirees and the deceased. The Great state of Arizona is largely Redneck, I mean Republican, and this is the other problem.

Rush Limbaugh enjoys an embarrassingly enormous devotee base in this State. For those not familiar with Rush, he is a bloated Republican mouthpiece and OxyContin end-user. To discover the finer points about the man please refer to: "Rush Limbaugh Is a Big Fat Idiot and Other Observations", written by Al Franken. Thank you, Al.

Sheriff Porcupino was in all his glory. With a big toothy grin, he cordially chatted and signed his name to whatever was handed him. The inmates enthusiastically fed his fat ego select words of worship. It was downright nauseating. This blowhard should be arrested for falsely impersonating a human being. I find his arrogance unsettling. His haughty sense of self-importance appears to contradict the integrity of his station as a civil servant.

The Sherriff was here to address the pigeon infestation problem and to do so in time to make the six o'clock news. True enough, the pigeons were beginning to outnumber the female inmate population. The problem had gotten so bad that the pigeons were required to submit flight plans to Prison Administrators. Many consider pigeons to be filthy flying rodents, but we girls love these birds. They were our trusted friends and our only reliable visitor. The jailed soon learn that friends tend to forget those who fortune forsakes. Adversity has a way of teaching us who our real friends are.

If Sherriff Porcupino stated concerns regarding the more than sixty infectious diseases (some fatal) that are associated with pigeon infestation, I'm afraid I missed that part.

He was more concerned with the fact that a number of dead pigeons were found in the yard. This was likely due to natural causes such as old age or the ingestion of prison food. Porcupino's line of reasoning was the following: The women in tent city were stuffing the pigeons with meth amphetamines and cocaine, which was causing the birds to die.

Oh boy. No self respecting crack whore is going to smuggle her drugs into jail via her most intimate of private parts for the sole purpose of plotting a pigeon's demise. Besides, everyone knows junkies don't share.

Porcupino's stand on this issue is congruent with his motto, "Reassurance through confusion".

As I listened to him babble on, at the dead center of my horror and disbelief, I thought, dementia is sad. It was tactlessly suggested by a fellow inmate that he was "brutally stupid and kinda creepy". This is possible and as irrelevant as was the purpose of his visit.

TWENTY-ONE

Cynophobia is the abnormal and persistent fear of dogs. I've got that. Some dogs, which when you meet them, remind you that despite centuries of domestication every dog is only one meal away from being a rabid hyena. Aggressive canines immediately sense my angst. They see me as an easy mark, something to be toyed with, or perhaps chewed. My apprehension stems from the multiple times I've been bitten while attempting to gain access to utility poles in backyard easements.

In nineteen years as a lineman-person, I've been bitten on four separate occasions with numerous near misses. When confronted by a menacing mutt, I experience an abrupt terror lasting at least a few minutes with typical manifestations of intense paralyzing fear.

"Doughy," shouted the guard making rounds. "Rollup, you're moving to the kennels tent."

Wide went my eyes in shock and incredulity. My rash decision to loosen myself from the grips of chain gang detail may have been premature. This reassignment was as disagreeable as is was unexpected, but I knew better than to object.

But the dog kennels? What the hell! Why can't they just put me back in the kitchen with my mouse friends? I looked to the tent ceiling for answers and wondered out loud, "this is some sort of a test, right?"

In what I knew would be a fruitless attempt, I approached the good officer who helped me blow the transfer request through.

"Excuse me, Officer." I said. My face was pale. I addressed her with the self-restraint of one who has just been told that they have one hour left to live.

"Is there a reason that I couldn't be assigned to kitchen duty?"

The officer tightens the lips and shakes her head solemnly.

"The chain gang officer was reluctant to release you."

191

I should've seen this coming. That old Ahole saw my leaving as a personal affront.

"The only way the officer would let you go is if you were assigned to the kennels, so I agreed. Sorry," she said with a sad frown.

"No, it is okay." I said with a weak smile. "I appreciate your help."

Typically, kennel work isn't assigned. It is a job divvied out on a volunteer basis. It is fair to assume that if a person doesn't work in the kennels than they'd rather not.

Those who are comfortable working with animals love working with the liberated canines. Many of these dogs, in particular the pit bulls, are rescued from situations where they were raised to fight for sport. It isn't unusual for kennel workers to return from their shift bloody and bandaged, yet eager to return. The dogs don't attack the inmates. The dogs attack each other. It is when a person tries to pull the dogs apart that they inadvertently get mauled.

Sheriff Porcupino's no-kill shelter was created to house and care for animals that have been abused or neglected by their caretakers. These are the Animal Cruelty Investigative Unit rescues. The kennels are located in the old jail in downtown Phoenixville.

On the drive to the kennels I noticed that things seemed rather laid back. Four of us are transported to the in an unmarked Ford Explorer. No cuffs, no formalities. The guard is real nice too. If I were not scared to death, I might be pleased.

The larger canines are housed on the top floor of a seven story high-rise. The smaller of the species are on a floor below. I was assigned to the top. This is good. I'd rather die quickly of a lethal bite to the jugular than endure the long slow bitter death of bleeding ankles.

There are a total of twenty-seven dogs on the top floor. I'm working alone. I'm certain there is a guard lurking about but I never see her. A list of work requirements and procedures are posted in clear view. All cells must be mopped with bleach water. Dog dew pickup is a never-ending task. Each canine is to be taken out of their cell for thirty minutes of interactive play. The roof is fully enclosed by chain link fencing and serves as a pleasant outside recreation area. It doesn't have real grass, it has that fake stuff, but the dogs don't seem to mind.

Feedings are at 0900 and 1700 hours. No more than one dog is allowed out of its cell at one time.

Ninety percent of the dogs on this floor are Pit Bulls. The American Pit Bull Terrier is a powerful square-headed monster with human eyes and a reputation for inherent viciousness. Most of these dogs have been bred for dog fights and are quick to brawl so -- You gotta keep'em separated.

A large majority of these Pits show outward signs of abuse. Physical scarring and an apprehensive shyness speak volumes about the environments they came from. Most have known brutality and unspeakable cruelty at the hands of those who gamble on their death.

These dogs had no intention of harming me. They were more afraid that I might harm them. The thought of this made me sad and then it made me mad. In the words of Victor Hugo: "First it was necessary to civilize man in relation to man. Now it is necessary to civilize man in relation to nature and the animals."

In the time it took to distribute the dry foodies, it was time to collect the empty bowls. These canines ate like starving orphans. Ethel was the exception. She was a middle-aged pit, gray and plump with big brown watery eyes. She could always be found in the same position on her blankee looking melancholy and rather pathetic with that big gray square head of hers.

Ethel would not touch the food in her bowl. Her girth told me that she did eat. Perplexed, I enter her cell and crouched down before her.

"Your foodies are over there," I said in baby talk pointing toward the bowl.

"Are you too fat to make the journey?"

Her soggy eyes didn't register a response.

I stood and retrieved the bowl. I placed it close to Ethel's monstrous head. Sitting cross legged in front of her, I gave her a nice smile.

Ethel looked at the bowl, then at me, and then she looked away as if in offense.

I narrowed my eyes examining Ethel's face for clues.

Without the assistance of a pet psychic, I find myself at a complete loss. I felt obligated to complete the task at hand and it seemed that Ethel has thrown a wrench into the works. I eyed her with some annoyance now. She eyed me back. We seemed to be contemplating each other, both of us at an impasse.

I turned my attention to the bowl of dry dog food.

"You know, Ethel, everyone is happy with these moist morsels."

I took a nugget out of the bowl, put it to my nose, and gave it a sniff. I'm a smeller. I can smell all things seen and unseen. My herculean sniffer told me that this dog chow was not so bad.

I popped the brown square into my mouth and bit down. For effect, as I chewed I rubbed my belly.

"Yummy, tastes like chicken."

Ethel watched attentively. Then I noticed her facial expression changed. Was that a smile? Dogs can't smile. Can they? It was as if she knew it really didn't taste like chicken and that I was an idiot. It was obvious that Ethel wasn't born yesterday. I may have met my match.

Meditating on my next course of action, I absently popped another kernel into the gullet. It really isn't all that bad. Add a dash of A-1 sauce and you've got a little something, something that could easily be served up to those pesky visiting relatives.

I slide the bowl under the bunk were Ethel could get to it later. She may be a closet eater. We were not allowed to leave foodies in the cells, but I didn't know what else to do. This is a problem that has to be solved by one shrewder than I.

When I got back to the tents, I asked the girls.

"What's up with Ethel? Why won't she eat?"

"Ethel won't eat out of a bowl," one of the girls explained. "She'll only eat food out of your hand."

"What're we running here, a daycare center?" I protest.

"Yeah, that's exactly what it is."

I suppose she was right.

The next day, I fed all the dogs and collected the bowls. Then I attended to Ethel. There she was on her blankee looking rather bloated and cute as a button. I checked under the bunk. The food in the bowl was untouched. I took it to the storeroom, dumped it, and piled the bowl extra high with some fresh stuff.

I returned to the cell and sat yoga style in front of Ethel. I grabbed a hand full of dog chow and held it close to her mouth.

Ethel extended her tongue touching the nuggets that stuck to its wetness. She drew her tongue inward and then daintily chewed the morsels. She was looking at me all the while with eyes that seem to say 'thank you'. It was the cutest darn thing I've ever seen. Now I know why Ethel is so fat. Mystery solved.

The dogs in this jailhouse kennel are darling and have a very sweet disposition. All they need is Love. My experience working here has proven to be curative. I'm no longer afraid of dogs.

The ItsHella County Sheriff's Office has an in-jail substance abuse treatment program. Substance abuse treatment is typically court ordered.

The program is an intensive six-week course which incorporates group therapy, a mandatory work program, anger management classes, employment readiness training and career counseling. The work program takes us to the local food bank. Here we assist in the production and packaging of emergency food boxes.

+++

It is 0800 hours ten of us are being transported, casually and unrestrained, in a Ford Econoline Van manned by some guy. We're headed to the Food Bank. The driver isn't a guard.

Remove the watchful eye of authority and the mice forget their good manners. As a Saint naturally seeks out the soul to save, the felon instinctively scans her surroundings for the next exploit. A couple days into this work detail, Mr. nice guy, who we will call Ned Flanders, was struck by the realization that he would have to exert some authority.

Ned exhibited all the personal power of a frightened fawn. In a feeble attempt to secure Alpha status, Ned called a meeting. Here he nervously read from a piece of, what might've been a Denny's napkin, a list of rules for which we women were expected to be in compliance.

The girls looked on in amusement as Ned stammered through his catalog of what seemed like absurd suggestions. One such decree, directed primarily at the Latinos, was that they speak English only. Some of the bilingual girls were in the habit of speaking amongst each other in their mother tongue.

Ned didn't know what the hell they were saying. This was making him nervous.

The women knew instinctively that it would not be prudent to encourage Ned to flex his managerial muscle. To observe his trifling dictates would surely be sending the wrong message. This isn't to say that Ned's demands were "blatantly" disregarded. A more passive-aggressive approach was employed. Ned was mollified, sucked up to, given the old oil, and generally made to feel that he was among friends and admirers.

Ned's improvised rules were soon forgotten. Surely he must've noticed, but he said nothing about it.

Uh-oh, there's your trouble. As is common knowledge to the average kindergartener, unenforced rules and idle threats open the flood gates to a free-for-all.

At the start of week two arrangements were made to have a predetermined supply of marijuana brought into the food bank. Although there was great promise of bundles of cash to be made here, I distanced myself from this caper. Cigarettes are one thing. Drugs are totally illegal.

A friend of a friend brought in the reefer delivery. The package was placed into the paper towel dispenser in the ladies public restroom. The women negotiated an hourly restroom break with Ned, stressing the requirement of our tending to feminine needs frequently. The subject matter seemed to make Ned squeamish. One might've thought we had asked him to run to the market and pick up a pallet of bloody tampons. Ned blindly complied with the girl's request.

A ridiculous amount of bathroom breaks allowed the girls the time required to break up the sack of reefer into vagina- friendly parcels. Packets the size of small eggs were wrapped in cellophane and assigned a mole.

We leave the Food bank at noon. When we return we're taken back to ItsHella intake unit. Here we're placed in a holding cell where we wait for a guard to escort us to a classroom.

Intake is the section of the jail where inmates are checked in and out. Court appearances, chain gang outings, and drug treatment participants are examples of the routine traffic. Additionally, newly processed inmates are placed in one of these holding cells while the powers that be decide where they will be placed.

They pull a kitchen worker to act as intake trustee. This trustee is required to issue clothes, bedding, and lame-o bags depending on the new arrivals purpose and destination. When a group files out a cell the trustee is required to clean it. Both men and women are brought into this section. Beyond this point it is primarily women only.

I routinely volunteered for intake trustee while assigned to kitchen duty. It is a job that often proved to be very entertaining. Checking out newcomers is a pleasant spectator sport. You never know when an old acquaintance might happen back for a revisit.

Occasionally, you'll get a newcomer who doesn't have the good sense to keep their trap shut. They are often full of piss and vinegar. Some are simply not cognizant of the seriousness of their current life situation. They scream and pound on the cell door demanding something to eat, drink, or a place to go potty.

There is a commode in three of these holding cells. The other three cells have none. Unlike the customer service department at Sears, screaming and cursing doesn't give way to better service. It was just this kind of blind ignorance that had a way of brightening my mood. Such exhibitions of rowdiness result in severe administrative retaliation. When guards become red faced it's time to grab the popcorn and get prepared for A Really Big Show.

These unrulies are dealt with severely. It would behoove new inmates to remember this catchy tune: You better watch out, you better not cry, you better not shout, I'm telling you why -- you'll get the chair.

Those who won't settle down are placed into a restraint chair. It is a chair with no legs. It is in the shape of a halved and hallowed out pear.

It weebles, it wobbles, but it won't fall down. It is made of a hard plastic. On the portion meant to support the back there exist plastic protrusions that cut into the spine.

The chair comes complete with onboard straps for the wrist, upper arm, waist and legs. The overhanging portion of one's legs are bundled together and strapped at the calves. If you're thinking "hogtied" you get the picture nicely.

Chair use requires a fair amount of man power. Usually four guards, one to a limb. These are four people who would rather be doing anything else and are noticeably peeved by the imposition. Four angry guards all foul breath distance away is a recipe for disaster. Things get ugly. Officers get rough and someone always gets hurt.

An inquiring mind may be wondering if these restraint chairs have ever caused any severe bodily injuries. If you consider death severe then the answer is yes. In the past there were two separate incidents where rough handling while being placed into the chair had resulted in fatalities.

Were wrongful death suits filed by the families?

You bet cha.

Both settled, one to the tune of eight and the other, nine million dollars. No worries though, it's no skin off Porcupino's bulbous beak. Arizona taxpayers picked up the tab. El Porcupino shamelessly advertises how his inhuman living conditions save taxpayers millions each year. The fact is this jail is hit with lawsuits at a rate exponentially higher than any penal institution in the United States.

Short confinement in this chair leaves its occupant meek and docile. Not surprisingly, restraint chair usage leaves the rest of the flock shell shocked and abruptly well behaved.

Because there were ten in our group, we occupied one of the three larger cells. These are the cells that have no toilet.

There is a fair amount of camaraderie within our group. We all have one very important thing in common, we will be released soon. Oh happy days.

The openness we experience in group counseling had the effect of a kinder more compassionate interchange between us. Of the ten women in the group, seven had been molested, preteen, by a father, stepfather, or brother. One story was more horrendous than the next. Each account was like a painting stolen from the museum of unbelievable cruelty.

In stark contrast, it might seem that I grew up in a Norman Rockwell painting. It is true that my family was in no way affectionate and had all the emotional availability of a pet rock. In fact, part of our souls had to be removed to make room for all the sarcasm. BUT, my God, this dysfunction was Shangri-La in comparison. These group sessions made it impossible for me to feel sorry for myself without feeling guilty about it.

We had been in the holding cell for about fifteen minutes. We were bantering back and forth cordially. All was pleasant and gay. That is until I noticed that Nancy was crying.

"What's the matter, Honey?" asked a woman in a soothing voice. The woman had an arm around Nancy's shoulder and was waiting patiently for a response.

Nancy seemed reluctant to say anything, but then just blurted it out.

"I have to go to the bathroom."

Kelly is sitting beside me. I like her. This woman is funny as hell. She's in here for embezzlement and should probably be in Federal prison but Mommy and Daddy are loaded. They paid big time to reduce her sentence to a wrist slap. Kelly and I were sitting side by side on a bench seat that was bolted to the floor. Our backs were against the cinder block wall. Nancy was about fifty feet away, closer to the cell door.

When I looked to Kelly, who was sitting to my left, she was already looking back at me. Her expression was an overstated smirk and her attitude was largely smartass.

One look at her sent a fit of hysterics rising up in me. It took an enormous amount of self control not to burst out laughing. If I had any sense I would've moved away from her. The thing is I like Nancy and this isn't a laughing matter. Not in this place. The more I reminded myself that laughing would be totally inappropriate, the funnier the thing became.

When an officer entered intake, Nancy rose grasping the bars frantically, her lower limbs twisted like a pretzel.

"Excuse me, Officer, I have to use the restroom, please, it is an emergency!"

The officer walked on by as if Nancy and her need didn't exist. This is business as usual in intake. What does this say about the psychological makeup of the prison guard? How is it possible that a human being of flesh and blood could regard another with complete and utter disregard?

When I worked as an intake trustee, I can recall two separate occasions when I had slid a green trash bag through the bars to inmates who had been in a holding cell for several hours without relief. In both cases the inmates used the garbage bag and were exceedingly grateful. As I mentioned, this isn't a laughing matter. It is an atrocity, appalling, and inhuman. How does this sort of willful neglect become habitual practice? That it continues, unchecked, boggles the mind.

Nancy knew better than to bother the officer further. As a last-ditch effort, Nancy pleaded with the trustee.

"Please, go to the office and tell them there is an emergency."

"They're not going to listen to me no way," said the trustee. "You best hold it and leave me out of this mess."

"Oh for God's sake," I chime in. "Just push a plastic trash bag through the bars. It won't take a second."

"No way, next thing you know one of you stupid bitches will have that plastic bag around your head trying to kill yourself. I ain't getting involved I told you."

"How about you don't give us that plastic bag," Kelly said, "and the ten of us find you in the yard later tonight and kill you? Do we need to remind you that there are about four-hundred women out there wearing the exact same outfit? Chances are you won't even be missed."

The trustee's eyes went wide.

"I ain't getting myself in trouble for none of you all."

Nervously she rose from her chair. We all watched as her ballooning ass disappeared into the supply closet followed by the sight and sound of a slamming door.

Nancy lost all hope for assistance. Frantically, she turned to the group.

"I have a medical condition, fecal incontinence. I have no bowel control. I can't hold it. I have to go, NOW!"

Her sense of urgency and the term 'bowel' sobered me to the core. I thought she had to pee. Intestines with a mind of their very own are an alarming proposition. Being trapped in a cell with aforementioned condition promises unthinkable horrors. We were all aware that Nancy frequently was excused from the classroom, but we never gave it much thought, until now. We all stared at Nancy feebly. There was nothing we could do.

"Use that newspaper," suggested one of the women.

There was a section of newspaper left behind by the last group. Nancy looked to us as if asking for our permission. As a group we concur.

I really hate this place. The humiliation Nancy was feeling was tangible. We all felt terrible for her. She placed the newspaper on the floor and dropped her pants swiftly.

In civility and for modesty's sake, we all stood and turned our backs to her.

The evacuation was volcanic, a nauseating repellent sound, a fetid bubbling and retching, as though her bowels were being flushed out with a fireman's hose.

The chill of the cell caused steam to rise from the deposit. The smell was appalling. I found myself sick to my stomach.

Nancy thanked us and apologized profusely.

No one said a word. We were all stunned. We buried our noses in our shirt collars and gagged at the stench. We stared expectantly at a wall clock whose minute hand seemed to be frozen in time.

Twenty minutes had passed before a guard showed up to escort us. This officer had a determined face, which, like most of the guards here, displayed power and incompetency in equal measure. When she got within fifty feet of the cage, her body recoiled as if receiving a karate chop to the throat.

"What in God's name?" She shrieked. Her face was a portrait of revulsion. She covered her mouth and nose with one hand.

With the toe of her canvas shoe, Nancy pushed the surprise package closer to the cell door. It didn't glide gracefully but was sluggish. It left behind a trail of slime.

The parcel movement caused a wafting of refreshed aroma. The officer looked at it and grimaced as if in pain. She scanned the group for an explanation.

We all wore a look of long endured world-weariness sprinkled with a touch of resentment. No one said a word.

"Trustee, HERE, NOW," screamed the officer. "Bring a pair of those disposable latex gloves. You're gonna need them."

The trustee sheepishly slinked out of the supply closet certain that she was in trouble for not being at the trustee's desk. Getting yelled at would be a treat compare to what the extreme near future had in store for her.

The officer, with one hand still palming her face, used the other hand to unlock the cell door.

While walking toward the cell, the trustee pulled on the latex gloves. She saddled up right beside the officer. Once she entered the zone, the mystery stench punched her right in the nose. Both latex gloves collided with the lower portion of her stupid face. HA, ha, I think she's going to be sick. The law of reciprocity was working its magic. Oh sweet compensation.

Pointing to the pungent packet, the officer ordered, "Get rid of that!"

The trustee followed the invisible line from the tip of the officer's finger to her newly assigned doodee.

The thud in the trustee's chest was palpable. The look on her face, priceless. The poor thing was overwhelmed with sickness and horror. The voice of one hundred Angels could not express our delight.

"NOW!" ordered the officer.

"Yes, Officer," the trustee's voice was an accordion of misery and dread.

This fortuitous turn of events lifted our communal spirits sharply. The atmosphere became suddenly buoyant. We were all feeling chipper than whatnot. A quiet excitement grew as we watched with finely tuned awareness as the trustee navigated toward her crappy chore.

We've been near that stink bomb for over twenty minutes and have become one with it. The trustee wasn't acclimated to the repugnance just yet.

With one hand she firmly and rather desperately grasped the lower portion of her face. The other gloved hand would do the important work of repositioning. Gathering three top portions of the splayed out newspaper the trustee began to lift what seemed to be a balanced load with her thumb and forefinger. This is a woman not without skills.

The trustee was a stout woman and frightfully thuggish. Tattoo's populated both arms like paisley spandex shirt sleeves. She also had tattoos on her neck disappearing into the hairline. This girl had more ink than a paper-mate manufacturing plant. She had the look of one who was hard core O.G. For those not hip on the lingo, this stands for original gangsta. She looked dangerous until she opened her stupid fat mouth. Then it became apparent that she was just a poser.

Although the newspaper gave it the old college try, it hadn't the fortitude to retain a wet loose stool such that Nancy could dish out. This was a payload that even a plastic bag might grimace to contain. As the trustee lifted, the newspaper began showing signs of weakness. At about the poser's knee, the bottom dropped out. BLAM-O! Hello cement slab, meet doodee! Just when you think things can't possibly get any better.

The trustees white doughy face turned ashen and then came the river of vomit.

OMG! Who could ask for anything more? To say we laughed would not be doing the thing justice. We roared. It was hysterical. This happy ending had worked out to be too much fun for any one mortal to expect or endure. It was the kind of uproar that turned to tears. Not all were so gay. Not the officer and certainly not, you know who. In good cheer we filed out of the cell one at a time each gingerly leaping over the height of depravity.

EPILOGUE

My release from county came with stipulations. I was required to comply with specific procedures outlined within a four-year probationary period. This included retribution paid to those I had stolen from. This amount was somewhere in the neighborhood of twenty-five hundred. It was divided up into monthly payments. All probation "client's" pay a fifty dollar monthly fee, which is a standard charge, added to what seemed like a long list of your fresh new financial responsibilities.

There is also a weekly random alcohol/drug testing. A daily phone call connects me to a recorded message which lets me know which colors have to report to the probation department that day to drop a U.A. My color will come up at least once a week, sometimes more. Standard drug testing cost eight dollars.

I'm also required to perform four-hundred hours of community service work. I bought a sewing machine and material from the Goodwill and methodically sewed a gazillion head scarves for the Cancer hospital. It took about four months.

A probation violation can have serious consequences. Probation is revoked and your original sentence invoked with immediate jail time.

I had twenty-four hours from the time of my release from jail to visit my probation officer. I stopped in nice and early to get this pressing matter out of the way.

When I entered his office my new probation officer was reluctant to acknowledge my presence. I take that back, he did grunt in response to my "Good morning, Sir." But he was too busy to actually look up. I've just emerged from an environment where people were routinely treated as subhuman and sub-intelligent. His discourtesy seemed a natural extension.

As I stood in the doorway I noticed that his desk was littered with brown file folders that were piled high and near tipping. Adjacent

205

shelving contained more of the same. There was a pack of Marlboro Reds on the desk. He had that stale cigarette smell.

Mr. Debag was a pudgy, ponderous gentleman with a pasty grayish complexion and the overall look of reprehensible health. His head was bald on top with a few choice strands sweeping left to right. His nose balanced a pair of black military rim glasses with smudgy lenses. He wore an off-white cotton shirt with hideous yellow stains about the pits. If this is a married man his wife needs a good talking to.

I stood silently in the doorway for what seemed like five minutes. This wasn't a good sign. I had ample time to take in every inch of him and his unkempt work environment. I wasn't impressed. He looked up, as if by accident, and cleared the vile mucus from his throat.

"Sit."

He was still reviewing my mighty plump file folder. I presume it is three convictions worth of girth. He didn't seem impressed. If he is a slow reader I could be here for days.

I was counting the stray hairs that littered the top of his greasy bean when he looked up suddenly.

Augghhh! I wasn't prepared for a full frontal at this proximity. I was struck by his fierce ugliness. I've seen better faces on a hemorrhoid.

His expression was dreary. His eyes were vacant like an unoccupied house that wasn't even interesting enough to haunt. He was tired, dead tired. I found myself squinting, looking intently for some sign of an inner light. Nothing was going on in there. The smudged lenses were making me nuts. I wanted desperately to hand him a Kleenex.

I smiled brightly hoping he might see that I wasn't as bad as my file suggested. Trying to engage him with the powerful pull of politeness, I rose from my chair, softened the eyes, and extended the obligatory hand.

"It is a pleasure to meet you, Sir." I lied.

The smile wasn't returned nor was the hand. This was the kind of welcome that prompted the old weary dread. Here again, I'm reminded of the scarcity of mercy and how we never find as much kindness in this life as we'd like. I knitted the hands together and sat back down. I was secretly relieved that I didn't have to touch him.

Mr. Debag looked down his vein riddled nose at me with a familiar contempt. This wasn't a happy man. I suppose if I looked like him I'd be gloomy too. It would appear that I was just another thing he had to do. He didn't have the good manners to pretend otherwise.

Speaking in a belittling monotone, Mr. Debag cataloged all my crimes and the consequential probation obligations.

"Chances are you'll end up right back in jail. The current recidivism rate is at eighty percent." Debag looked down at his pack of cigarettes, he needed to light up. "Do you know what that means?" He asked speaking to me as if I were a retarded lost cause.

"Your dismal point of view doesn't discourage me, Sir. I'm not going back to jail. I hope this news doesn't further dampen your already murky spirits."

Debag looked at me with blatant indifference.

"We'll see about that. Get out of my office."

This miserable splotch wasn't very encouraging. Eighty percent recidivism, I think I know exactly what that means. Tax payer dollars are being funneled into a "correctional" facility that receives a yearly boost in its budget in spite of a touted eighty percent failure rate. This is a racket that thrives on return customers.

I began looking for employment immediately. An effort to get back into my field of expertise, telecommunications, was a no-go. I was advised that a notable amount of time needed to pass before my reentry was to even be considered. I was politely told that they might be interested in talking to me in about seven years. Seven seemed to be the magic number where making a decent wage was concerned. This I understood and half expected.

I narrowed my job search to accommodate my new life situation and my temperament: manual labor, outside work, no supervision, and a four-hour work week. HA, just kidding about the hours, sort of. And obviously, my new employer must have a lenient policy regarding the hiring of convicted felons.

The very next day, I hit the streets with résumé in hand and a look of humble desperation. I responded in person to an ad for a tow truck driver. I found myself at a company that specialized in vehicle impounds and repossessions. They hired me with zero experience.

I had been forthright regarding my recent release from jail and probation obligations. They exhibited a complete lack of interest, as if I had merely provided proof of a necessary prerequisite. I was to start the next day, eight sharp. Perfect! I shook the hand of the woman who hired me.

"Thank you so much," I said. "You won't be disappointed."

I turned away and in a sudden rush, the full realization of what just happen swept over me. My thoughts sang Hosanna. I gave a yell, and a jump, and started off in a run. I had a job. I had a "real" job! I called my Mom with the good news.

I was starting all over from scratch. I had no clothing, furniture, or money. Until my wages began to come in, I was obliged to live in the narrowest way. Necessities I'd acquire in time, all purchased second hand. This would be my lesson in dignified poverty. I'll become so thrifty that the fumes in the air from nearby restaurants will nourish me. In true Zen form, I'll lack everything and want for nothing. It is in times like these that it is best to take the big, broad, spacious view. Did you know that there are as many different ways of going without money, as there are of spending it? Focusing on what you lack is rarely beneficial. Instead, I'll bear in mind that I have exercise, all the free fresh air I can stand, and a place that I can come to and go from at will. No more locked doors.

With the start up cash provided by my Mother, I moved into a low income neighborhood that was located a healthy bike ride away from my new job. The small one bedroom apartment had no heat, no air conditioning, but there was a swamp cooler. The swamp cooler is a common phenomenon here in Arizona. During July and August they are as pointless as an ashtray on a motorcycle.

The apartment building was of cinder block style construction on a poorly maintained lot. Its amenities included a small deposit, low-rent, no credit/background checks, no English, no questions, no problems.

Perfecto! I laid out cash in the amount of $200.00 for a cleaning deposit and $400.00 for the first month's rent. I completed the transaction with a heartfelt gracias.

I received on the job training in the art of vehicle impounds and repossessions. This company had a reputation for being unscrupulous. Police were called daily to mediate for angry vehicle owners. Unjustifiable impounding, unreasonable storage fees, and damage to the vehicles were some of the chief complaints.

The nine year old company was owned and operated by a couple in their sixties who were active participants in the 24/7 rigors of the operation. They were devote Mormons and treated me like their daughter. It was month two of my new hire status when I received a call from the boss.

"Janie, now don't get upset. I need you to bring your truck to the yard. There are a couple of detectives here with a warrant for your arrest."

I did get upset but kept my emotions under wraps. Now what? When I got to the yard, two detectives and a female officer met me. I was cuffed, placed into the back seat of a cruiser, and taken to the nearest police station.

It wasn't until I found myself in a holding cell that I broke down, the tears flowing like a river. Here we go again. Here we go again.

I wasn't behind bars long. My boss put up $3,000 cash for my bail and I was back to work within an hour.

 The warrant was for a crime I had committed two years ago. It was a charge they held back just for this occasion. I wasn't surprised. I was half expecting this. They do this routinely.

I witnessed this happening several times to girls who were released from jail. They take two steps out the door and are arrested on "so called" new charges. These new charges are weighted with the fact that you have "priors" now. This translates into prison time. I was looking at a minimum of six years. It was time to get a lawyer.

My Mother and my Brother, Eddie, helped me with lawyer's fees. It cost $15,000. This amount was split three ways, my portion paid in monthly payments. Thank God for family. I plead guilty to a charge of trafficking stolen goods, adding another felony to my list of folly. I paid associated fines, but wasn't required to serve additional time.

I was a lousy repossession agent. I was okay so long as I hooked the vehicle unobserved then disappeared. However, if a single mother came running out of the house crying, followed by a gaggle of confused children, I was done for. A sight never failed to reduce me to tears. I'd stop the truck, drop the vehicle and give it back with instructions on how to make it repo-proof.

At four years past my release from jail, I was still driving a tow truck, but moved away from the repossession and impound industry. It is too depressing.

Long-term exposure to this type of work, collections, produces an angry, toxic workforce. This unwholesome environment was renting space in my head and disturbing the all-important inner peace. Toxic coworkers are bad for our mental and spiritual health.

In 2010, I had the very good fortune of landing an excellent job working for a towing company who was contracted out by Triple-A to run service calls. It was a good job.

Two years into this position, AAA issued a notice to all contractors stating that each driver must undergo a background check. Everyone who had a felony within the past seven years was fired. I was one of several.

And so you see, much like the tattoo I had placed on my forearm on impulse decades ago, a felony is equally, vividly, chillingly permanent.

Tow Truck drivers with a solid work history and good references find work easily, as did I. I intend to continue this work until I become a well-known and celebrated Author – God willing.

I moved to a better apartment in a nicer part of town. It is a smaller, humbler place than I'm formerly accustomed. I like it. I live alone, simply and well within my means.

I don't leave my home without first dropping to my knees and thanking my creator for his/her perfect love and my perfect life. Am I all better? Hardly, I'm not who I need to be but Thank God, I'm not who I used to be.

Today I'm a happy girl. Because I'm an earthbound mortal, everyday isn't skittles and beer. However, when it rains I don't mind. I've got blue skies on the inside.

What I learned from my experience in jail and the shameful antics, which put me there, can be best summed up in the words of the late and very great Franklin D. Roosevelt. "These dark days will be worth all they cost us, if they teach us that our true destiny is not to be ministered unto, but to minister to ourselves and to our fellow men."

Thank you for reading my story. May the author of all things bless you and make you an instrument of peace spreading love where ever you go.

29821137R00121

Made in the USA
Charleston, SC
25 May 2014